CW01671606

To Jonna

Great working with you.

Old School Perspectives on Taekwon-Do

Ciarán McDonald M.A., M.Ed.

Old School Perspectives on Taekwon-Do

ISBN 978-1-9161135-1-0

Printed in the United Kingdom

First Printing, 2019

Printed and bound by Printondemand-worldwide UK

Published by Old School Perspectives Media

Apt 29805

Chynoweth House

Trevissome Park

Truro TR4 8UN

www.osperspectives.co.uk

ISBN 978-1-9161135-1-0

9 781916 113510 >

Warning

The techniques contained within this book can be dangerous if not practised under the supervision of a qualified and insured instructor. If an individual attempts any of the techniques contained within this book without the supervision of the aforementioned instructor, then it is the responsibility of the individual to assess their own risk and capability to do so and any resultant loss or injury will be the fault of the individual. Neither the author nor the publishers can accept any responsibility for any injuries sustained when practising the techniques contained within this book.

Acknowledgments

I can never thank my wife Sunaina and my two tiny children Tiernan and Anoushka enough. Writing a book takes lots of time. Writing one whilst working fulltime and bringing up children means making sacrifices to carve out the time necessary to write. My wife and my children have had to sacrifice their husband and father in order to permit the completion of this book. They have been very patient and understanding and deserve so much more than mere thanks.

Thank you to Hanshi Patrick McCarthy for inspiring me in my Karate studies. Hanshi McCarthy is the most knowledgeable authority I have met on Karate kata and their applications. He is a truly impressive individual and a few hours in his company feels like a lifetime of study. I am honoured to have been accepted as an instructor in his organisation.

Thank you to the Chairman of P.U.M.A. Taekwon-Do Master Ray Gayle and Vice-Chairman Master Mark Ogborne for teaching me the beautiful art of Taekwon-Do and for permitting me to run my school the way in which I believe it should be run. I am proud to be part of such a great organisation.

Thank you to Barry Fisher, David Wilson, James Burchell, Jack Holloway and Marcin Borawski for acting as uke in my classes and photos.

Thank you to a whole host of people whose courses, seminars, books and DVDs have kept me on the right path over the years: Iain Abernethy; Rory Miller; Gavin Be Becker; and Stuart Anslow to name but a few.

Lastly, thank you to Funakoshi Gichin and General Choi Hong Hi. Two men of small stature but huge character, who worked tirelessly to achieve great things. Without their desire to keep their respective cultures alive, neither Karate nor Taekwon-do would exist today. And the world would be all the sadder for it.

About the author

Ciaràn began his martial arts journey at the age of ten studying Shotokan Karate. After the inevitable hiatus through his teenage years, Ciaràn took up martial arts again in 1999 when he developed a passion for Taekwon-Do. During this time he has studied:

- 'Freestyle Taekwon-Do'
- W.T.F. TaekwonDo
- I.T.F. Taekwon-Do
- P.U.M.A. Taekwon-Do.

After being awarded his black belt by P.U.M.A. Taekwon-Do, Ciaràn set out on a mission to find out the applications to the Chang-Hon tuls he had been studying for so long. After attending many seminars of Bunkai experts like Iain Abernethy, Ciaràn briefly studied application-based Shotokan under author Andi Kidd. Ciaràn also studied classical Jujutsu at three different schools where he picked up essential skills in throwing, falling and joint locking. In 2011, Ciaràn discovered 'Old School Karate' in the form of Koryu Uchinadi (KU). Ciaràn gained his black belt in KU in 2015 and was granted a Shidoin Teaching qualification by Hanshi Patrick McCarthy 9th Dan in 2016.

Ciaràn is head instructor at both Didcot Old School Karate Jutsu (which opened in 2015) and Oxfordshire Taekwon-Do (which opened in 2011). Ciaràn continues to travel and study all types of martial arts. He has studied as a member of Newbury Brazilian Jujutsu since 2016 and currently holds a blue belt in the art.

Ciaràn is an expert in education and has taught at many of the UK's leading universities. He holds a Masters of Arts in Language Teaching and a Master of Education in Educational Research. It is this background in education and academia that has guided Ciaràn in crafting his approach to the analysis and scrutiny of all things Taekwon-Do.

Contents

Foreword by Patrick McCarthy

9th Dan

Since beginning Karate more than fifty years ago, I have been intrigued by kata, which remain for manysomething of "*a riddle wrapped in a mystery inside an enigma.*" The practical application of these abstract routines have always held a fascination for me. Kata represent the essence of Karate-do and are regarded by many as, 'time capsules' of sorts, giving those with the eyes to see, a glimpse into the mindset and practices of an ancient culture and their secret art of self-protection. It is ironic, however, that though kata are the common thread, which weaves together the very fabric of this art, they are still widely misunderstood and misinterpreted.

In 1985, after nearly twenty years of training, I became discouraged by such misinterpretation and related incongruous practices. It wasn't that I disliked what traditional karate represented, it was that I could no longer accept its modern interpretation, of kata! As such, I began to search for a teacher, a style, or even an organisation that could mentor me in a more rational, coherent and systematised manner. My search and related travels permitted me to look outside the box and rediscover 'old school' traditions and related practices once considered the lifeblood of the art before its rapid expansion as a cultural recreation and rule-bound competitive sport. After many years of study, at the sources of origin and with many of its most senior authorities, I was able to collate, restore and systematise many of these old-school practices back into a functional application system. Based almost exclusively on 2-person application practices, and being mindful to pay homage to the cultural heritage of this art and its original pioneers, my late Okinawan master [Kinjo Hiroshi] helped me name this pathway, '*Koryu Uchinadi*' [[古流沖手] or '*Old-School Okinawan Fighting Art*'.

Ciaran McDonald has been a member of our organisation, the IRKRS (international Ryukyu Karate Research Society) and a student of Koryu Uchinadi since 2011. In this time not only has he demonstrated a fundamental understanding of the principles of old school karate but has wholly embraced the values and practices of our organisation. In recognition of this dedication and study, I awarded him a Shidoin teaching qualification in 2016. Therefore, it is exciting for me to see him use this knowledge of these principles and practices to interpret his first love, 'Taekwon-do'. I am so very pleased to see how these 'old school' methods have helped empower him, breathe new life into his art and serve as an effective tool to analyse other traditional fighting arts, including Taekwon-do.

This book is well researched, informative and though respectful, does not shy away from the controversial questions. As an author and historian I am enthusiastic about balancing the physical study of ones art with an academic element. This book will help those studying Taekwon-do who also seek such balance.

Patrick McCarthy
Hanshi 9th Dan
IRKRS Director

Foreword by Stuart Anslow

5th Degree

When I first started Taekwon-Do at the beginning of the 90's, a block was a block, a punch was a punch and no-one ever questioned it. To be honest, most never realised that the patterns we practiced were so much more in-depth than we knew. Most, but not all that is.

All of the books that detailed Taekwon-Do at that time contained little to no details of applications for the patterns beyond the standard 'a block is a block' variety, though there were a few Masters that looked beyond that, such as Willie Lim and B. S. Huan. It was Master Lim that gave me my own insight into the patterns of Taekwon-Do being more than the sum of their parts (via a 2 or 3 page magazine article on some of the movements that was published in the early 1990's) and I came to find later, that Master B. S. Huan did similar as well. Thus I started my own research, culminating in the release of my own books on applications, *Ch'ang Hon Taekwon-do Hae Sul, Vol. 1* (with Volume 2 following a few years later, after further research).

Today, whilst a lot of students are still content with performing patterns in their basic form for tournaments, gradings or even simply fitness, others want a more in-depth and rounded art, the key to which, lies in the patterns themselves, which Ciarán has concluded, much like I did and much like Masters Lim and Huan did before us.

The movement for more realistic applications to our patterns has grown as the years have gone by, as well as my own, there are a few more books on the subject matter available (though not enough sadly, which is why this book is very important), magazine articles regularly appear on them and there are the odd blog posts about them, each one opening the eyes of more and more students to the possibility that their art is more than they knew and thus can be better.

'Old School Perspectives on Taekwon-Do' by Ciarán McDonald is another important step in the right direction, not only for the student of Taekwon-Do but for the art itself, as its still sorely needed.

What's more, is that Ciarán's background in both Karate and Taekwon-Do gives him the perfect vantage point for his research as, as most know, Taekwon-Do's father art was Shotokan karate and many of the moves and combinations of the patterns are derived from the kata's of Shotokan.

Whilst we have taken different approaches within our respective books, we have reached many of the same conclusions, which in my opinion gives both our views and research deeper validation. That said, Ciarán's work offers some different perspectives and much food for thought as well, as he discusses key concepts contained within the patterns, what is required for movements to be practical, as well as why they actually are already, as well as detailing some of the least understood movements that some of our patterns contain, such as Joong-Guns U-Shape block.

'Old School Perspectives on Taekwon-Do' is a joy to read, not only as it's a subject close to my heart, but it is well thought out, researched thoroughly and presented well and whilst I may have done a lot of research myself into this area I picked up some more information and techniques to add to my own, already fairly extensive, toolbox, when it comes to the performance, practice and realistic application of our Taekwon-Do patterns and I have no doubt that this book will become an important addition to every Taekwondoins library.

Stuart Anslow 5th Degree

Author

Editor in chief - *Totally Taekwon-do Magazine*

태권도

태권도

Old School Perspectives on Taekwon-do

Ciarán McDonald M.A., M.Ed.

Introduction

The success of Taekwon-Do represents the reality of one man's dream. A sickly child who studied Karate under his colonial masters, 'the Japanese', Choi succeeded against all odds to create a Korean martial art with global success. This art became the beautiful Taekwon-Do that we practise today. Like all the most successful martial arts, Taekwon-Do has become specialised to occupy a niche in that it has become 'the kicking art'. As such, it has further become the undisputed world leader in kicking. No one kicks like a good Taekwon-Do fighter. The art has developed a set of mechanics that attempt to incorporate science in order to generate power whilst maintaining the ancient principles of posture, focus and breathing. It has created a dynamic sport, which permits people to test their skills in a safe and regulated environment whilst its rules facilitate the performance of many of the flamboyant kicking techniques that make the art unique. Finally, it offers students 24 stunning choreographed routines of self-defence against an imaginary opponent called 'tuls'. Tuls are the main content of this book.

The performance of tuls is a meditative exercise; it is a chance for introspection. Many tuls require a level of physicality that takes years, if not decades, to achieve. The never-ending quest to achieve perfection of the tuls can be seen as a direct expression of the 'Do' (or 'Tao' in Chinese). This metaphysical concept encapsulates the human struggle to find meaning in the universe and therefore achieve individual wisdom. Though, for many, the patterns represent a requirement to progress through the ranks or a chance of acquiring a medal or competitive status, for most, the 'Do' has become the main focus of the patterns' performance. For most people, what the patterns look like is far more important than what they contain. There is nothing wrong with this. However, this book is not for those people. This book is for those who are seeking to find out more about what the patterns mean and how to apply them.

The Chang-Hon Tuls represent a rich resource of techniques that one can use to learn to defend oneself against the common acts of violence perpetrated by aggressive attackers. They contain efficient methods of dealing with all manner of expressions of violence and offer a variety of responses which include (but are not limited to): throwing; joint locking; choking; pressure points; escaping; controlling, striking; and, of course, kicking. However, to the uninitiated, recognising the presence of many of these techniques is very difficult. This is because most were incorrectly labelled as 'blocks' before they were inherited from Shotokan Karate; the art studied by General Choi in Japan. Taekwon-Do has, like modern Karate, become a block, kick, punch art. These three constituents have become the perspective through which the applications of the patterns are now understood.

This situation has been further compounded by the publication of General Choi's *Encyclopaedia*. In both the 15-volume version and the condensed version, the General has offered 'surface level' explanations of the applications of the tuls. He did **not** openly state that these were the only possible explanations. However, owing to the hierarchical structure of Eastern martial arts, it is seen as disloyal to question what the General has written. This has prevented many from openly stating (and hence exploring) the possibility that there may be more to this than meets the eye. Indeed, the incorrect assumption perpetuated by the block, kick, punch model is that violence takes place at unrealistic distances. This misconception is embodied in the modern practice of set sparring.

Set sparring, with its ritualistic approach to violence, has helped to obscure the plethora of close-quarter fighting techniques present in the Chang-Hon Tuls. The main focus of set sparring is blocking and countering prearranged attacks from long distance using blocks in a manner that they were never designed for. However, set sparring is a modern practice created in the 1930s by Japanese university students with little or no experience of real-world violence. It was based on the ritual of Kendo and was never a method used in ancient times to train the ancient techniques contained within the patterns. Therefore, it is possible for us to look beyond it and its modern assumptions. Indeed, if we want to find out what the patterns mean, we have to first find out where they come from. Only then can we ask ourselves: "How is it that the originators of these techniques envisioned using them? What kinds of violence did they expect to encounter most?"

For many, especially the Koreans with their memories of the horror of the subjugation of their people, accepting that much of Taekwon-Do was inherited from Shotokan Karate is a bitter pill to swallow. However, it is undeniable that many of the templates contained within the Chang-Hon Tuls came from the Shotokan kata, which themselves were derived from ancient Okinawan versions (heavily influenced by Chinese Kung Fu). It is essential that we understand our own history if we are to understand our own art. It is for this reason that Chapter 1 will explore the influences of Karate on the formation of Taekwon-Do and specifically the role that Karate kata played in the creation of the Chang-Hon Tuls. Chapters 2 and 3 will then go on to look at two of the major constituents of Taekwon-Do training: blocking and stances. Here, it will attempt to show how these two major constituents of 'traditional' martial arts have been mistakenly maligned by many within the so-called 'reality arts'. By re-examining the purpose and method of both blocking and stances, we will see that both elements can provide the student of Taekwon-Do with essential devices that help negotiate all manner of violence. It will be shown through the exploration of blocking and stances that the Taekwon-Do patterns also provide effective methods of dealing with violence at all three ranges: kicking, striking and grappling.

This book is not a challenge to the legitimacy of Taekwon-Do but rather an auxiliary resource that will offer those with enquiring minds a new avenue of study. It is hoped that the knowledge contained within this book will strengthen one's understanding of Taekwon-Do and will elevate the patterns once again to a position where they are the student's first choice of combat-ready responses to real-world violence. If this book can in some way add to the student's enjoyment and understanding of our great art then it will have been worthwhile.

Taekwon

Ciarán McDonald M.A., M.Ed.

Chapter 1: The Okinawan elephant in the room:

An analysis of the influence of Shotokan Karate kata on the Chang Hon Tuls

Almost since its inception, Taekwon-Do has portrayed Karate as anathema. General Choi, creator of the International Taekwon-Do Federation (ITF) and the father of modern Taekwon-Do, along with many other prominent Taekwon-Do revisionists, has attempted to deny the influence of Karate on the development of Taekwon-Do[1]. When placed in the historical context of Imperial Japan's subjugation and systematic rape of the Korean culture and people, it is hardly surprising that any Korean of that epoch should wish to distance themselves from anything Japanese. Indeed, post-war 'Koreanisation' saw the Koreans rebrand many things Japanese; often inventing histories to show derivation from Korea rather than the hated old imperial masters. Karate, the basis of Taekwon-Do, was such a practice to become appropriated. The removal of Karate from the Taekwon-Do story left a void which was to be filled by overstating the contribution made by the indigenous foot fighting art of Taekyon[2]. This created the plausible myth of Taekwon-Do being a wholly Korean art, developed over millennia, with a heritage directly traceable to the ancient and legendary warriors of the Hwa-Rang. Such a historical revision was to fit well with Korea's post-World War II nationalistic fervour. Nevertheless, Taekwon-Do's use of Karate kata made its denial of Japanese heritage less credible; prompting Choi and his team (most of whom held blackbelts in Shotokan) to design the Chang-Hon (Blue Cottage) series of tuls. Though distinct from the Karate kata, the new tuls contain many long sequences (templates) that are so similar to those contained within Karate kata (and especially the Pinan/Heian series) as to make the origin of their source undeniable. However, the Taekwon-Do tuls were not crafted in numerical sequence; nor were they designed all at once. Furthermore, though the early tuls appear to be based on Karate kata, many of the later tuls can be seen to shift in defensive strategy and display more of the flamboyant kicking techniques present in Taekyon.

1 When asked in an interview about the influence Karate had on the development of Taekwon-Do, Choi stated "Almost none" despite publicly recognising the links between the two arts earlier in his life (see Gillis, 2008).

2 Ouyang (1997) and Gillis (2008) show that the research used to authenticate Taekwon-Do's historical linage was disproved by historians. Furthermore, they show that Taekyon is very distinct from Taekwon-Do and more akin to a game than a martial art that can be used to maim and kill.

This chapter is an attempt to explain the influence Karate kata had on Taekwon-Do tuls by exploring the historical parallels between the development of Karate and Taekwon-Do. It will also attempt to illustrate the derivation of Taekwon-Do from Karate by comparing the first 13 Shotokan kata to the first 9 tuls (coloured belt) to show similarities and developments in set defensive sequences, often referred to as templates.

A Short History of Karate

Karate originates from Okinawa: one of the Ryukyu Islands, which was once an independent archipelago Kingdom (Wikipedia [1], 2011). Though much of Karate history is vague at best, it is known that Okinawa had its own indigenous form of martial arts. This was a plebeian form of grappling called 'tegumi' (McCarthy, 1999). Okinawa had very close commercial and cultural ties to China and, through cultural exchanges, many southern Chinese came to visit or live permanently in Okinawa. Among these migrants were martial artists probably versed in some of the southern styles of Kung Fu prevalent in their homeland. Incorporating Kung Fu, Okinawan martial artists were able to transform their own indigenous art into a more complete discipline, which became known as 'Toudi' or 'Te' (sometimes referred to as 'Tang Te' (唐手); meaning 'Chinese hand'). Among these styles, White Crane Kung Fu and Monk Fist Boxing are widely believed to have been the most influential on the development of what was eventually to become Karate (Cohen, 2017). It is interesting that, though the Japanese were to sever cultural ties with the Chinese, Karate masters still viewed China as the place to go for martial arts training. Indeed, Chojun Miyagi, founder of Goju-Ryu Karate, was known to travel frequently to China to continue his martial arts education, more than 300 years after the introduction of Kung Fu to Okinawa (McCarthy, 1999).

Figure 1: A map of Okinawa and the Ryuku islands

Figure 2: Ankoh Itosu

The next significant milestone in the development of Karate was the invasion of the Japanese in 1609. This was to see the enactment of laws that initially would ban Okinawans from carrying or owning weapons and eventually from practising martial arts (Abernethy, 2002). Fear of inevitable punishment if caught was to encourage Okinawans to practise Karate in secret and away from the gaze of spies or informers (Funakoshi, 1988). Such secrecy was to add much to the mythology and mysticism of Karate.

One popular myth was that another consequence of the Japanese occupation was the unification of many of the Toudi schools in resistance. Though this historical event has been widely disproved, the myth purports that such a unification inspired the Okinawans to defend themselves against armed attackers using rudimentary fishing or farming tools. It also claimed to have transformed the empty-handed art of Toudi into an extremely violent and brutal method of dispatching attackers.

The year 1903 saw the public demonstration of Karate, and the shroud of secrecy was lifted. The next great development in Karate was Anko Itosu's creation of the Pinan/Heian series of kata. These kata, whose exact derivation is much debated, appear to be a distillation of classical kata. They represented a modernisation of Karate, existing as a structured and progressive syllabus. Inspired by the health-promoting properties of Karate practice, and in an attempt to keep Okinawan culture alive, Itosu oversaw the introduction of Karate into the Okinawan school system (McCarthy, 1987). Teaching Karate to children was to necessitate many essential changes in the name of safety. First was the occlusion of many of the lethal or potentially maiming techniques. To achieve this, most techniques were simply renamed as blocks or punches; mislabels and resulting misapplications that persist even today (Abernethy, 2002). Next, the emphasis on two-person drills was changed to 'Kihon' or basic line work in order to accommodate large classes (McCarthy, 2012). Lastly, and most importantly, the in-depth study of the applications of the kata, known as 'bunkai', was withheld. These changes made Karate a more callisthenic-based pursuit and removed the worry of children misusing it to maim or kill their school friends (Burgar, 2003).

It was during this period that many of the Japanese cultural practises we associate with Karate were ushered in and established as traditions. Though many contributed to the formation of Karate traditions, it was Yabu Kentsu (1866–1937), one of Itosu's primary instructors in the Okinawan public schools, who instigated many of the militaristic practices common to most modern dojos (Madis, 2003a). Yabu used his experiences of serving as an officer in the Japanese army whilst stationed in China to create a number of innovations designed to assist the instruction of the children. These innovations included:

Figure 3: Yabu Kentsu

- bowing upon entering the training hall;
- lining up students in order of rank;
- opening class with specific formalities or signs of respect;
- seated meditation (a Buddhist practice further developed in Japan as a result of 'Kendo' ('way of the sword' [Korean: 'kumdo' or 'influence']);
- sequenced training, including warm-up exercises, fundamentals, forms and sparring practice;
- answering the instructor with loud and respectful acknowledgement; and
- closing class with formalities similar to opening class.

(Cook, 2001: 26–28, 52–53; Donahue, 1993; Ryozo, 1986, all cited in Madis, 2003a)

So successful were these new methods of discipline that they were taken up by many of the Okinawan pioneers teaching in Japan, including both Funakoshi and Mabuni. Though some of these practices were present in the military-derived martial arts of Judo and Kendo, they were not present in Okinawa nor in China prior to Yabu's introduction. Furthermore, it has been asserted that neither were they witnessed in any of the Korean arts prior to Yabu (Madis, 2003a). It is important to note that this development represented the first substantial effort to impose a universal standard on Karate. It has been remarked that, prior to its inclusion in the school system, Karate was a haphazard art that was highly subjective. Not only did it lack a formal syllabus but also it was extremely individualised and esoteric (McCarthy, 2012).

The next major development in Karate was its introduction to the Japanese university system. In 1912, the Japanese Imperial Navy docked in Okinawa for a week of naval manoeuvres. Officers and enlisted men were so impressed by the defensive capabilities of Karate that they were loudly complimentary of it on their return to Japan (Croft, 2009). This led to a call for a delegation of Okinawan Karate Masters to travel to Japan and give a demonstration in front of the Butoku Kai (Japan's leading martial arts authority) (McCarthy, 1999). The delegation was led by Gichin Funakoshi, a former student of Itosu. Funakoshi, a short man, had been a weakling as a child and his parents had arranged Karate tuition in the hope of improving their son's physical condition (Funakoshi, 1975). Little could they have dreamt of the effect that this would have on the young boy's future because Funakoshi, under the tutelage of Master Azato and Master Itosu, was to become a gifted and highly influential martial artist, who would later become the 'founder of Shotokan Karate'. Furthermore, he is now widely recognised as 'the father of modern Karate' and, though not solely responsible for introducing Karate to the world, he was by far the most successful at popularising it. He achieved this by introducing it to the Japanese mainland and teaching it throughout Japan's university system.

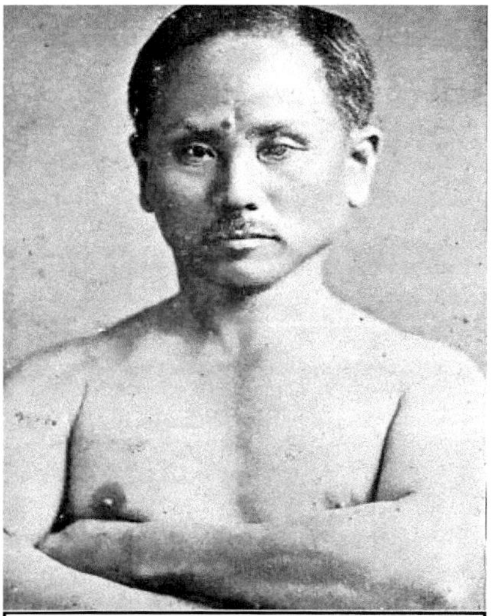

Figure 4: Funakoshi Gichin

However, it is thought that Funakoshi, unbeknownst to the Japanese, chose to continue teaching the new 'children's version' of Karate. This was alluded to by the famous Karate fighter and sworn enemy of Funakoshi, Choki Motobu. Motobu publicly accused Funakoshi of being an imposter whose Karate, although elegant, was ineffective (McCarthy, 1999). According to Motobu, Funakoshi had no idea of Karate's application, but relied on "tricky behaviour and eloquent explanation." Ironically, though Funakoshi was teaching a much-reduced syllabus, the transformation to modern Karate was not yet complete and he still taught many of the close quarter grappling techniques that would eventually disappear altogether from the Shotokan syllabus (Abernethy, 2012). Indeed, in his early books, the keen observer can witness photographic evidence of throws, chokes, ground work and joint locks (Funakoshi, 1935); techniques that have been removed from modern Shotokan. Nevertheless, it is known that many of the kata applications were withheld and therefore other material was needed to fill the gap. Kata became the perfect solution. Soon, learning kata became a measure of progression through the ranks. Unfortunately, most of the old masters, including Funakoshi himself, only knew a few kata. So, Funakoshi began importing kata from other sources (Burgar, 2003). Soon, knowledge of the defensive principles of kata was replaced with aesthetic qualities of performance; prompting many stylistic changes such as the lengthening of stances and the heightening of kicks (Abernethy, 2012).

During the 1930s, Japan's leading martial arts association, and home to many of its leading military minds, the Butoku Kai, laid down strict conditions that Karate must satisfy in order to achieve official recognition alongside the other martial arts such as Judo and Kendo. These criteria included the following:

1. The creation of a grading system: Karate ultimately adopted the grading system of Jigaro Kano, the founder of Judo, who developed progressive coloured belts, or kyus, as a method of motivating his students.

2. The adoption of a uniform: Karate eventually decided on a lightweight 'gi': a white training garment also introduced by Kano. Traditionally, Karate students just wore loose clothing and, in subtropical Okinawa, as many of the historical pictures of the founders of Karate can attest to, often bare-chested training was common.

3. A safe method of training: the Japanese initially viewed Karate training as too dangerous and haphazard. This prompted many innovations in Karate training, including the development by Kenwa Mabuni and others of rudimentary padded sparring protection.

4. The development of a sport: Karate was required to create a competitive method of testing the fighting skills acquired through instruction. This innovation was to fundamentally change the focus of Karate instruction for the next 100 years as the close quarter methods of Chin-Na and Toudi were to make way for the long-range tactics inherent in this new and highly popular sport (McCarthy, 1999).

Figure 5: Dai Nipon Butoku Kai

However, though Okinawan Karate influenced the Japanese, the Japanese also shaped the form of modern Karate forever. During the period of Karate's introduction, Imperial Japan was extremely nationalistic and used racial supremacy to justify its military aggression. Therefore, the Karate ideogram that indicated Chinese linage had to go. In place, the new name, although pronounced the same, would no longer mean 'Chinese hand' (唐手) but would become 'empty hand' (空手) (McCarthy, 1999). This then rebranded Karate as a wholly Japanese art, which could then be taught to Japanese youth. On its introduction to Japan, Karate was to become more militaristic, with kata instruction and practice involving huge numbers of students and resembling marching more than the one method of Okinawa. Furthermore, it has been said that, contrary to expectations, the Japanese military feared that their recruits were using Karate fighting skills to brawl amongst themselves and so the army did not broach the combative applications of Karate, preferring to use it as a method of improving physical fitness alone (Croft, 2009).

Following the end of World War II, it was this radically modernised and Japanised form of Karate that was to be brought back to America by soldiers stationed in Japan, and was to be further exported to nearly every country in the world. Interestingly, although the Okinawans envisaged using Karate to keep their culture alive, the new modern form of Karate was pervasive and all but eradicated the original Toudi-based Karate so dear to them. However, perhaps the most influential factor in the transformation of Karate from its roots as a secretive brutal civilian defence system to an art form that is enjoyed by millions worldwide was the success of sport Karate.

Figure 6: Kata training at Shuri Castle

From its inception as a criterion of recognition by the Butoku Kai, the sport side of Karate provided the final vehicle to usher in the radical changes that would forever obscure kata applications. Because many of the new Karate schools either deliberately avoided teaching kata applications or didn't understand them, many of the young males who studied Karate required a method of utilising some of the 'killer' techniques they were learning in the abstract form of kata and of burning off some testosterone. The sport version of sparring or 'Kumite' filled the gap for many and thus became the third constituent 'K' in Karate's Kata, Kihon and Kumite programme. However, the rules of Kumite favoured certain techniques such as lunge punches and high kicking, which promoted long-range fighting. Furthermore, the sport often precluded the use of close quarter techniques such as grabbing, gouging, throwing and grappling. Therefore, although the new sport effectively utilised many of the techniques practised in Kihon (basic line work), it did so at a distance that made many of the kata techniques ineffective. Since the success of the Kumite techniques could be judged 'effective' by the results they generated in this rule-bound combat, many of these young men began to favour them over the then abstract techniques contained within the kata, which defied explanation and proved ineffective in this new form of combat. Thus, sporting Kumite became the lens through which much of the efficacy of kata was viewed.

With this new perspective established, kata techniques were also viewed as responses to long-range attacks. This position was further strengthened by the creation of 'step sparring', which, heavily influenced by the ritual of the Japanese Budo culture, always began with the attacker outside attacking range but closing the space with a single determined attack (invariably accompanied by a vocal warning or 'ki ai'). This new form of combat fitted well within the existing Japanese culture and, indeed, the new model was far more akin to the strategy of Kendo than that of the Okinawan fathers. However, the creation of the sport form of Karate was probably largely responsible for the success the art has achieved. Now, Karate is enjoyed by millions worldwide and is a much more inclusive art form than at its inception. However, in the immortal words of Funakoshi himself: "It is a long way from the Karate that I learnt when I was a child in Okinawa" (Funakoshi, 1975).

A Short History of Taekwon-Do

In the beginning there was Karate. Though some Koreans would definitely have learnt this art in Korea, it seems that many of the founders of the major kwans (gyms or schools) learnt their Karate in Japan through the university system set up by Funakoshi and his peers. Of the many schools to emerge at the end of World War II, the five most influential (and from which most others were spawned) were referred to as 'O Geh Ki Kan'. These were:

1. Chungdohwe (later called the Chungdokwan).
2. YMCA Kwanbop bu (later called the Changmookwan).
3. Songmookwan.
4. Yunmookwan (later called the Jidokwan).
5. Moodukwan.

(Kang & Lee, 1999: 98, cited in Madis, 2003a)

Figure 7: Lee Won Kuk's Chungdokwan

The most significant of the kwans in the development of Taekwon-Do was probably Lee Won-Kuk's Chungdokwan. It is here that Choi Hong Hi was to study, teach, and eventually be presented with the opportunity to start his own school.

It is thought that Lee Won-Kuk may have been the first Korean to learn Karate. Lee studied in Chuo University under both Gichin

Funakoshi and his son Gigo (Burdick, 2011). It is not certain when Lee began his Karate education but it is estimated to be during the early 1930s (Madis, 2003a). However, according to GM Yong Taek Chong (a student of Lee), Lee may have begun his study in secret whilst still a teenager. After being formally recognised as the most senior Korean student of Karate and licensed to teach, Lee returned to Korea and set up Chungdokwan in 1944. His schools were very successful and many of the key figures of Taekwon-Do became his students. As Lee has said;

> "*The lessons were popular and many people wanted the training. We had to be careful to recruit and keep only the best, most highly motivated students. The students we kept included some of the prominent figures in modern taekwondo. We worked hard to keep up the quality of instruction and our students, and to promote tangsoodo as a positive influence in Korean society. Our main objective was to instill discipline and honor in young people left without strong moral guidance in those troubled times.*" (Lee, 1997, cited in Madis, 2002).

However, Korea was very politically unstable during the turbulent post-war years and Lee's popularity was to prove his undoing (Ibid).

As Lee's student base grew into the thousands, he was approached on behalf of the president and dictator, Syngman Rhee. Lee was offered a post in Rhee's government as Minister of Internal Affairs if he could guarantee Rhee the votes of all his students. Lee, recognising the corruption of his honour that such a move would have caused, politely declined. Rhee promptly declared Lee a Japanese spy and collaborator, forcing him and his family, after release from prison, to eventually flee to Japan. This accusation was particularly ironic because, according to historians: "83% of 115 cabinet ministers were Japanese agents or collaborators under Japanese colonial rule" (Lee, 2002, cited in Madis 2003a). The disappearance of Lee prompted many of his senior students to start their own kwans. One such school was Choi Hong Hi's Ohdukwan.

Figure 8: Syngman Rhee

Choi, the father of Taekwon-Do, like many Koreans before him had studied Karate whilst in Japan. He had attended high school, in Kyoto, and then graduated in law from Chuo University (the same university where Lee Won-Kuk studied under Funakoshi) (Madis, 2003b). Choi, like Funakoshi, was a short man who, as a child, was physically weaker than his peers (Choi, 2000).

Figure 9: Choi Hong Hi

To escape a local bully and to improve his physical condition, Choi took up Karate (an Okinawan art, practised by many Koreans during the Japanese occupation but widely seen as belonging to the reviled Japanese). After the end of World War II, many of the Korean kwans who specialised in Karate continued to teach it; some under the new Japanese name of 'Karate' (meaning empty hand), but others, like Lee Won-Kuk, under the Korean pronunciation of the original Chinese characters (唐手： Tang Soo Do). The Tang referred to the Chinese dynasty and gave the connotation of Chinese, rendering the meaning (like the original Okinawan version) 'Chinese Hand Way' or 'Way of the Chinese hand'.

Though originally there were many 'schools' of Karate, four emerged from them to become the 'major' or 'main' styles. These were: Shotokan Ryu, Goju Ryu, Shito Ryu and Wadu Ryu. Most of the Taekwon-Do pioneers had studied Shotokan; this being the most successful at self publicising. In fact, Nam Tae Hi, General Choi's technical advisor and the father of Vietnamese Taekwon-Do, had also learnt Karate directly from an old pupil of Funakoshi, and Choi himself is said to have journeyed across Japan to meet with the revered father of Shotokan (Gillis, 2008). It was therefore Shotokan that Choi taught to his jailers whilst under sentence of death (an act that saved him from execution) and later to both Koreans and Americans in a post-war Korea (an act that may have secured his many promotions). However, Choi was to resent promoting the culture of his old colonial masters and "realized that we needed to develop our own national martial art, superior in both spirit and technique to Japanese karate" (Gillis, 2008). It is ironic that Choi, as with many others, should wrongly identify Karate with Japan because its origins lay in a country that has many historical parallels to Korea. For example, both Okinawa and Korea were invaded by the Japanese; both at some point considered China to be the cultural capital of the educated and well bred; both suffered bans to their martial arts; and both were eventually to use martial arts in an attempt to assert cultural identity.

Once Choi had decided to 'Koreanise' Karate, the first thing to go was the name. Although the martial art was not to change substantially for some time, the name would have to reflect the post-war nationalistic fervour that was sweeping Korea. Both names, the Japanese 'Karate' and 'Tang Soo Do' with its obvious Chinese connotations, would finally give way to the name championed by Choi and reluctantly supported by the less than convinced right-wing president of South Korean, Syngman Rhee (University of Leicester Taekwon-Do Club, 2011). Choi had chosen Taekwon-Do (meaning foot fist way) as the new name due to its resemblance to the name of the ancient Korean foot fighting game of Taekyon. However, this name was not popular with Rhee. Rhee, who had witnessed a demonstration in September 1954 of Choi's 29th infantry division performing Karate techniques, was so impressed that he sanctioned the teaching of this art form throughout the entire Korean army. However, so as not to provoke any anti-Japanese sentiment in the less than stable Rhee, he was told that he was witnessing the ancient foot fighting game of Taekyon (Gillis, 2008).

It took Choi a long time to get Rhee to accept the new name of Taekwon-Do. However, once he had achieved this, he was able to use it as leverage over the heads of the other major kwans, many of who were opposing the rebranding. Nevertheless, Choi was very astute in recognising the need to Koreanise Karate. He had already started to tinker with the stances and hand positions of Karate in an attempt to improve and remould in Korean form and was keen to link his improved Karate to something Korean in origin. As a result, Choi commissioned research that would link Taekwon-Do to Taekyon and would give historical credence to the 'plausible myth' that Taekwon-Do was not in fact derived from Karate but was actually the descendent of the almost extinct practice of Taekyon. Unfortunately, this was a hard sell to those 'in the know' because Taekyon was predominantly a game derived from the martial art Subak, which was thought to have been banned under the Koreyo Dynasty due to it encouraging gambling among civilians (Wikipedia (4), 2011). Although, Taekyon, or Subak, were definitively Korean in origin, and was depicted in many famous paintings of national heritage, it was decidedly different from Karate, for example, Karate was created as a close quarter civilian defence system designed to brutally disable the types of 'thieves and roughians' one would expect to meet while walking through the dark countryside carrying wages or takings from sales at market. In such an encounter your survival or the survival of your family would depend on quick and decisive victory. Therefore, Karate contains an array of techniques such as: elbow strikes; hand strikes; attacks to vital areas; and powerful kicks that are not present in the more sportsman-like Taekyon (Gillis, 2008).

Choi's research quickly established the history that he needed to prove the derivation of Taekwon-Do from Taekyon and, although the validity of this research has been roundly disproved, its findings remain the basis of the legend of 'the Korean Martial Art of Taekwon-Do' to this day (Burdick, 2011).

Problematically, there was still the thorny issue of the kata, which remained predominantly the Pinan/Heian series, created by Ankoh Itosu and popularised by Funakoshi and his peers. In fact, some stalwarts, attached to the name 'Tang Soo Do', split from the major kwans, ensuring the continuity of Tang Soo Do. Many of these schools, to this day, continue to practise the

Pinan/Heian series whilst supplementing them with weapons-based kata. However, the use of Karate kata presented a definite threat to the myth of Taekwon-Do's Korean linage and so Choi set about designing his own kata, or 'tuls', as they are known in Korean. It should come as no surprise that Choi and his first technical advisor, Nam Tae Hi, both Karate students, should look to Karate when seeking inspiration for his new Korean kata. Indeed, there is such commonality between the first **new** Taekwon-Do tul (Hwa-Rang) and the Heian series that a charge of plagiarism would be hard to defend. Therefore, despite Choi's claim that Karate had 'almost no influence' on the development of Taekwon-Do, the contrary would seem obviously true.

This is a bitter pill to swallow for many Taekwon-Do practitioners who are heavily invested in the 'Korean myth'. But it is important that we can accept this if we are to ever look beyond the given and apply a questioning critical mind to the applications of the Taekwon-Do patterns. It is for this reason that this chapter will attempt to map the development of Choi's Chang-Hon, or Blue Cottage, series of tuls on to the first 13 Shotokan kata. Though there is no way of knowing which kata Choi and his advisors knew, it can be speculated that, as a 2nd degree black belt in Shotokan, Choi would probably have had a working knowledge of the first 13 Shotokan kata. Therefore, one would expect to see these influencing the design of the Chang-Hon Tuls.

The Chang-Hon Tuls

Throughout the late 1950s and the 1960s, Choi, with the help of many contributors in the form of technical advisors (including Nam Tae Hi and CK Choi), was to create the majority of his new tuls._Though many believe that the 24 (later to become 25) tuls were created in sequence, they were anything but. In fact, the first tul, 'Hwa-rang' (number 8 in the Chang-Hon series) was designed by Choi and Coronel Nam Tae Hi in 1956 (Anslow, 2009), though it has been suggested that it was developed at early as 1952 (Forest East Taekwon-Do, n.d.). Its name was to appeal to a Korean sense of historical pride by invoking images of the legendary Hwa-Rang fighters: elite warriors and scholars of a bygone era. This was a powerful and skilful invocation that would help legitimise the myth of Taekwon-Do's Korean ancestry[3]. Therefore, it is ironic that Hwa-Rang Tul should be based so heavily on the Heian (H) series and most notably the H Sandan kata. The

3 A tertiary comparison of Karate and Taekwon-Do is all that is necessary to establish the similarities. Stances, blocks, punches, kicks and many of the cultural practices of both arts are so similar that it is obvious that they are derived from the same source. When you compare Karate/Taekwon-Do with other arts such as Judo or many Kung Fu styles, it is clear that both defensive strategies and body mechanics are so dissimilar that they are distant relatives at best. It would be easy for a Shotokan Karate student to train in a Taekwon-Do dojang and vice versa, without the need for radical adaptations. This would not be true for a Judo or Kung Fu student.

second tul, Choong-Moo (number 9 in the Chang-Hon series), was also a collaboration between Choi and Nam. Named after the 16th-century naval genius, and scourge of the Japanese Navy, Admiral Yi Sun-Sin, this tul was a further attempt to historically legitimise the new Korean art. Indeed, all further patterns would take the names of historical Korean figures, many of whom battled against great odds to further the cause of Korean cultural identity and independence. Chronologically, the next patterns in the series were Ul Ji and Sam-Il Tuls (Choi, 1959). Created by Choi with the assistance of Sergeant Han Cha Kyo and CK Choi, respectively, these tuls were third and fourth in creation despite both being black belt patterns, with Sam-Il a 3rd degree tul and Ul Ji a 4th degree tul. These four patterns were published in Choi's first publication in 1959. This book did not reach a worldwide audience because it was only ever printed in Korean.

The four new patterns were also accompanied by the lost pattern U-Nam (sometimes called Woo-Nam). The fate of this pattern was again an example of the fickle nature of post-war Korean politics and their influence on the developing art of Taekwon-Do. U-Nam was a pattern that was named after the then right-wing president Syngman Rhee; the title being Rhee's pen name. However, Rhee was forced out of power and into exile in 1960, just one year after the publication of the book. Though not stated by Choi, it would have been political suicide for the general to promote a pattern with the same name as the persona no grata ex-president, and so U-Nam, like the president, was exiled.

The capriciousness of Korean politics was to determine the setting for the development of the remaining Taekwon-Do patterns. After his participation in a military coup d'état in 1961, Choi was to fall foul to the purges of the new president, General Park Chung Hee. Choi was subsequently forced to resign his military commission and was appointed to a diplomatic post in Malaysia (Choi, 2000). It seems that most of the tuls (16 in total) were created by Choi with Sergeant Major Kim Bok Man and Woo Jae Lim during Choi's exile in Malaysia. This meant that, by the time of the publication of Choi's first book in English on Taekwon-Do, in 1965, 20 tuls had been completed and were therefore featured.

All the remaining tuls (bar one) were to be finished by the 1972 publication of the *Taekwon-Do Encyclopaedia* (Anslow, 2006). The last and most controversial pattern, Ju-Che, was to appear during the early 1980s. This pattern was to replace Kodang and made a total of 25 tuls. Named after the political thesis and doctrine of North Korean leader Kim Il-Sung, the term 'Ju-Che' was seen as offensive by many Taekwon-Do instructors, who associated it with the Stalinist politics of North Korea. The rejection of North Korea on ideological grounds often resulted in a complete rejection of the new tul or an acceptance of it whilst retaining the old name of Kodang.

As has been shown, the tuls were not created in the order they appear in the syllabus. Therefore, it is difficult to understand what logical sequence, if any, could have been envisaged for the complete series. However, like Itosu's Heian series, some of the first Chang-Hon Tuls can be seen (more or less) to progress in difficulty. For example, the Chon-Ji Tul, the first in the series, contains only 19 moves, consisting of three techniques and two main stances. Whereas Dan-Gun, the next in the series, contains 21 moves, still with only two main stances, but the footwork and techniques become more involved. However, Toi-Gye Tul and others such as Po-Eun are not consistent with such a model of progression. Toi-Gye contains many more moves (37) and seemingly more complex techniques than Hwa-Rang Tul (the next in the sequence). Whereas Po-Eun Tul, which bears a striking resemblance to kata Tekki Shodan, appears infinitely easier than Choong-Moo Tul.

The Kata

The kata we are interested in are the ones that General Choi and the other pioneers may have encountered whilst studying Shotokan Karate. These would certainly be the Heian series of five kata. It is impossible to say with any degree of certainty what supplementary kata these Koreans were taught. All we can do is use the syllabus of modern Karate as a guide. Therefore, the first 13 kata have been selected for comparison with the first 9 tuls. There is much discrepancy with the order in which these kata are taught and as such a single (though not necessarily correct) source has been used as a guide (Trimble & Morris, 1995). It is highly likely that General Choi and his technical advisors, as black belts in Shotokan, would have been familiar with many, if not all, of these kata and therefore they will be examined to check for similarities and modifications. These kata and corresponding tuls acan be seen in **Table 1**.

The Taikyoku kata and the Saju series of fundamental exercises

The Taikyoku kata are a series of training kata developed by Yoshitaka Funakoshi, the son of Gichin Funakoshi. It is thought that they were created as a method of preparation and practice for the student before he/she embarks on learning the 'real' kata. In Taekwon-do the Saju series can be seen to occupy a similar position and have a similar function. The Taikyoku series originally consisted of three kata which were labelled 'Shodan, Nidan and Sandan respectively. These are contained in Funakoshi's original version of 'Karate-do Kyohan' where he describes in detail the methodology and purpose. However, the series was later expanded into seven at a much later date. All three original kata are very similar in nature. For example, all the kata contain:

- Blocks and punches in isolation

- All are based on the pattern diagram of Pinan/Heian Shodan (an step shape like Do-San)
- Each turn is accompanied by a block and each block is followed by a single strike
- A requirement of the student to go up and down the middle
- Three punches in a row (like Dan-Gun Tul)

The term 'Taikyoku' is taken to mean 'first cause' and the meaning was described by Funakoshi as having a special spiritual significance. However, the Chinese kanji used for the name Taikyoku are pronounced as 'Tai Chi' in Chinese, which translates as 'Grand Ultimate'. The kata are as follows:

Taikyoku Shodan – Consists of just two moves: a low block and a middle punch. Both are performed in a karate front stance (walking stance).

Taikyoku Nidan – The same as 'Shodan' except the middle punches are replaced with high punches.

Taikyoku Sandan – This kata differs in that, like Chon-ji, it has a series of middle blocks in back stance (L-stance).

These initial training kata proved so popular that the other main styles of karate either adopted some or all of them or as in the case of Goju-Ryu, developed their own versions. What is interesting is that, by creating and adopting these kata, Karate had ultimately accepted kata as a method or training techniques rather than practising techniques already learnt elsewhere. These kata therefore represent the final move from a partner-based system to a solo orientated system where drilling in large numbers was the dominant pedagogy.

Order	Kata	Tul
0.	Taikyoku kata 1-3	The Sajus
1.	Heian Shodan	Chon-Ji
2.	Heian Nidan	Dan-Gun
3.	Heian Sandan	Do-San
4.	Heian Yondan	Won-Hyo
5.	Heian Godan	Yul-Gok
6.	Tekki Shodan	Joong-Gun
7.	Bassai-Dai/Sho	Toi-Gye
8.	Kanku-Dai/Sho	Hwa-Rang
9.	Empi	Choong-Moo
10.	Sochin	
11.	Jion	
12.	Jitte	
13.	Ji'in	
x	Chinte	

Table 1: A list of the Shotokan kata and possible source of templates in the Chang-Hon tuls

Key Terms

We shall now concern ourselves with the analysis of the patterns. However, before we do this, we must precede this with what academics refer to as 'defining terms'. That is to say, taking a term that is key, but which is ambiguous in meaning, and deciding on a definition for purposes of clarity. The constituent parts of kata/tuls are as follows:

- **Techniques:** punches blocks, kicks, etc.
- **Templates:** short combinations of moves.
- **Kata:** long choreographed sequences designed as mnemonics containing many templates.

1. Techniques

These are the smallest components of a kata. They include punches, blocks, kicks, strikes, releases, etc. This is often the level of focus used when interpreting kata bunkai, leading to limited interpretations.

2. Templates

These are two or more techniques combined into short sequences, for example, front snap kick double punch. These set combinations, referred to by Karate scholar Hanshi (9th Dan) Patrick McCarthy as 'templates', are defensive sequences of actions which have been evolved to deal with many of the most common types of physical violence likely to be perpetrated by an unskilled fighter. Some of these templates are reactive, whilst others are proactive. Though most of the techniques have been mislabelled simply as blocks and strikes, it is important to realise that the same movements have almost infinite applications. For example, waving your forearm backwards and forwards could be used for anything from applying 'wax on/wax off' to conducting the London Philharmonic. Therefore, the application of a technique depends on context. Furthermore, the templates, like the proverbial clock, represent combinations of techniques that transcend the simple block-punch-kick paradigm and offer endless applications amounting to so much more than the sum of their parts. Therefore, it is highly probable that simple techniques, looking so much like blocks and punches, when combined may represent a whole array of defensive strategies, including:

- locks and holds;
- chokes and strangles;
- throws and grappling;
- escapes and evades; and
- many of the essential (though unsportsmanlike) recourses such as biting, gouging, butting, scratching and spitting.

It is also important to note that many of these templates exist in most martial arts. Therefore, they are common property. For example, front snap kick double punch is an instinctive attacking template whose origins are sure to be prehistoric. It is only when the templates are combined as kata that issues of authorship become relevant.

3. Kata/Tuls

Kata consist of numerous templates stuck together end to end. The original purpose of kata was to record the principles inherent in an individual's fighting system so that a master could pass them on and that a pupil could remember them. Therefore, in an age before cameras, video, computers, etc., they represented an efficient mnemonic or aide memoir.

The place that kata would have occupied in traditional training is hotly debated. It is commonly thought that kata would form the basis of a syllabus. Once the student had perfected the techniques and body movements herein, the secrets of the kata would then be revealed. However, Patrick McCarthy has controversially proposed that kata would represent a culmination of the drills and sparring a student would have already engaged in. In this model, the kata would be used as a solo form of training, available when a partner was not. Though it may be impossible to say which model is historically correct, with early Taekwon-Do/Karate classes sometimes being upward of 400 students, it is easy to see how a 'learn kata and wait for revelation' model of instruction may well have been the only pedagogy possible.

Analysis

The tuls that follow are the ITF Chang-Hon (Blue Cottage) series, as penned by General Choi Hong Hi and technical advisors. The techniques (moves) alluded to in the analysis represent the techniques as they appear in the Taekwon-Do tuls ('TKD' hereafter in this section) and **not** as they appear in the Karate kata ('K' hereafter in this section). Only the first nine tuls, the coloured belt tuls, will be analysed here. Because there is much variation of the kata within Karate and its various styles, we shall be using the Shotokan versions as they appear in Trimble & Morris (1995). Furthermore, though there will be inevitable differences between the kata and the tuls, we shall focus predominantly on the similarities present.

1. Chon-Ji Tul (19 moves)		
This is the first tul learnt in TKD. It consists of two parts, the first representing the heavens and the second representing the earth. Therefore, it encompasses the duality of Eastern philosophical concepts such as ying-yang (or 'um-yang' in Korean). The tul involves a number of 90- and 180-degree turns; each turn starting with a block and ending in a stepping middle punch. It includes only three techniques: middle punch; middle inner forearm block; and low outer forearm block. It appears to be most influenced by the kata Heian Shodan.		
Kata	Common Moves	Description
Heian Shodan	1,2,3,4,5,6 (7,8)	90° turn low block; obverse punch
Taikyoku Sandan	9–17 (modified)	180° turn and low block; obverse punch

Notes:

1. Heian Shodan, like Chon-Ji, is the first form taught.
2. The whole sequence of moves 1–8 is then repeated (9–16) replacing low block with middle block.
3. Moves 1–6 follow the exact sequence or Heian Shodan. Moves 7 and 8, though the same techniques, are additional.
4. Chon-Ji is based almost entirely on Taikyoku Sandan containing all the same techniques and almost identical patterns of movement. However, the Taikyoku contain no backward stepping.

Chon-Ji Tul 19 Moves

0

1

2

3

4

5

6

7

8

9

10

11

12

13

14

15

16

17

18

19

2. Dan-Gun Tul (21 moves)

Named after the legendary founder of Korea, this is the second tul in the Chang-Hon series. Though there is much repetition in this tul, we are introduced to twin forearm blocks, rising blocks and knife hand guarding blocks (KHGBs).

Kata	Common Moves	Description
Taikyoku Nidan	5, 6, 7,8	90^0 turn into low block, 3 x stepping high punch (270^0 turn)
Heian Shodan	14, 15, 16, 17	4 x rising block
Heian Shodan	13, 14	Low block/rising block combination
Heian Shodan	18, 19, 20, 21	270^0 turn, KHGB, stepping high punch, turn 180^0 KHGB, stepping high punch

Notes:

1. Rising block in move 14 in K is with an open hand and appears to be more of a parry and a preparatory move than a hard block.

2. Moves 18–21 have been modified from the K version but they are very similar and contain exactly the same turns that they are unmistakably derived from Heian Shodan. In the K version, 18 and 20 are low blocks and 19 and 21 are middle punches.

3. Dan-Gun is very similar to the Taikyoku series throughout. It has a central column with two lateral sequences either end. Each lateral sequence, like Taikyoku Nidan, consists of a block and a high punch.

Dan-Gun Tul
21 Moves

0

1

2

3

4

5

6

7

8

9

10

11

12

13

14

15

16

17

18

19

20

21

3. Do-San Tul (24 moves)		
Named after the legendary educator and independence campaigner, Ahn Chang-Ho, Do-San Tul appears to be based largely on Heian Sandan and Heian Yondan, although the same sequences are contained in other kata too (Kanku-Dai and Jion). However, the high outer forearm block, seen in moves 1, 3, 10 and 11, do not appear in any of the first 13 kata.		
Kata	Common Moves	Description
Heian Sandan	4,5,6,7	Flat fingertip thrust midsection; release; 360^0 turn back fist
Heian Yondan (and Jion)	13, 14, 15, 16 17, 18, 19, 20	Wedging block; front snap kick; double punch (repeat on other side)
Jitte	21,22,23	2 x rising block and 270^0 turn
Ji'in	23,24	2 x sitting stance knife hand strike

Notes:

1. Moves 4–7 vary only slightly from the K version. The first move is different: in TKD it is a KHGB and in K a double forearm block. However, there are distinct similarities: both techniques start with a 90^0 turn and both start with the hands sweeping from chamber across the body and ending with one hand in front of the solar plexus whilst the other remains midsection and out in front. Also, both K and TKD perform this technique in an L-stance.

2. Moves 4–7: another interesting difference is the release move and 360^0 turn. In K at the midpoint of the turn (180^0 through) the spear hand is held against the back, indicating that at this point it is still trapped and that the 360^0 turn is an essential part of the release. This is a departure from TKD where the release move is believed to occur before the turn.

3. Moves 4–7: though the last move of the sequence differs in each art, they both finish with a spinning side strike (K=side fist/TKD=back fist).

Do-San Tul 24 Moves

0

1

2

3

4

5

6

7

8

9

10

11

12

13

14

15

Do-San Tul
24 Moves

16

17

18

19

20

21

22

23

24

태권도

4. Won-Hyo Tul (28 moves)

Named after a famous Buddhist monk who successfully proselytised to much of the Silla Kingdom during the 7th century, Won-Hyo Tul is almost a carbon copy of kata Heian Nidan. It contains many of the same techniques, and a great many of the long sequences (templates) are performed in the same order.

Kata	Common Moves	Description
Heian Nidan	1,2,3,4,5,6	Twin forearm block; inward knife hand strike; fixed stance punch; turn 180^0 (repeat, i.e. 4, 5 & 6)
	7,8,9,10,11,12,13	Bending ready stance; middle side kick with high section punch; 3 x KHGB, spear hand & 270^0 turn
	13, 14, 15, 16 17, 18	Sequence repeated from earlier (1–6)
	19, 20, 21, 22, 23, 24	Circular block; front snap kick; land in walking stance; reverse punch (repeat sequence)
	25,26,27,28	Bending ready stance; middle side kick with high section punch 270^0 turn; guarding block; 180^0 turn guarding block

Notes:

1. Moves 2 and 5 in TKD are inward knife hand but in K they are upward punch, i.e. Hwa-Rang. However, the finish positions are identical apart from the open hand in TKD and closed in K.

2. Move 7: bending ready stance in the K version keep the toes on the floor rather than at the knee joint. Furthermore, the K version brings hands to the hip rather than in a guarding block.

3. Though both K and TKD turn 180^0 on move 7, both arts face opposite directions.

4. Move 27 is 180^0 turn in K and both 27 and 28 are KHGB in K.

Won-Hyo Tul
28 Moves

0

1

2

3

4

5

6

7

8

9

10

11

12

13

14

15

Won-Hyo Tul
28 Moves

16

17

18

19

20

21

22

23

24

25

26

27

28

태권도

5. Yul-Gok Tul (38 moves)

Named after the great philosopher and scholar, Yi I, Yul-Gok Tul appears to be mostly original in design. Though it contains a sequence from Heian Yondan, the source of the remaining sections of Yul-Gok do not appear to be the first 13 Shotokan kata. Therefore, it may be safe to assume that Yul-Gok is mostly the work of Choi, et al.

Kata	Common Moves	Description
Sochin	1,2,3 and 5,6,7	Slow punch extended sitting stance; double punch (repeat other side)
Heian Nidan	7,8,9 and 11,12,13	Middle inner forearm block at an angle; front snap kick; landing in double punch (repeat)
White Crane Hsing	15,16,17,18,19,20	Hooking block; reverse hooking; block punch (repeat)
Heian Yondan	22,23,24,25,26,27	Bending stance guarding block; side kick with high section punch; land as elbow strike into opposite palm (repeat sequence)

Notes:

1. Moves 22 and 25: in K, the bending stance has both hands at the back hip rather than in a guarding block (as in TKD). This is the second tul to make this same adaptation. Therefore, the authors (Choi, et al.) obviously strongly favour this technique over the K version. It would seem that pulling the hands to the hip has a hidden significance when considering the application of the technique. Therefore, it dispels the TKD myth that the bending stance is merely a preparatory stage for the kick.

2. Furthermore, though the hands of each bending stance appear radically different, both K and TKD start the technique by standing side on and initially pulling the hands across the body in preparation.

3. Moves 7–9 are identical to K. However, TKD version finishes in double punch; not single.

4. Though not one of the first 13 kata (so technically beyond this study), Sochin is on the Shotokan syllabus and is therefore a likely source of inspiration for Choi, et al's tuls.

5. Moves 15–20, though not present in K, exist in a White Crane Hsing. So, the derivation, though beyond this study, is still interesting.

Yul-Gok Tul
38 Moves

0

1

2

3

4

5

6

7

8

9

10

11

12

13

14

15

Yul-Gok Tul
38 Moves

16

17

18

19

20

21

22

23

24

25

26

27

28

29

30

31

Yul-Gok Tul
38 Moves

32

33

34

35

36

37

38

6. Joong-Gun Tul (32 moves)

Named after the hitherto unknown assassin of the Japanese Governor General of Korea, Hiro Bumi Ito, (Ahn) Joong-Gun Tul appears to be mostly original work.

Kata	Common Moves	Description
Heian Godan	30	90^0 turn into closed stance angle punch
Bassai-Dai Jitte	31, 32	U-shaped block (x2)
Chinte	7,8,9,10	KHGB; slip front foot to upward elbow strike (repeat)
Empi	27, 29	Low palm pressing block (x2)

Notes:

1. Move 30, 90^0 turn and angle represent two moves in K.
2. In K, moves 31 and 32 contain further moves in-between the two U-shaped blocks. However, these are positions that are transitioned through when moving from 31 to 32.
3. Though not one of the first 13 kata (so technically beyond this study), Chinte is on the Shotokan syllabus and is therefore a likely source of inspiration for Choi, et al's tuls.
4. In TKD, the palm pressing blocks start from a guarding stance. In K, they do not but in fact come one after the other without interruption in a sequence of three.

Joong-Gun Tul
32 Moves

0

1

2

3

4

5

6

7

8

9

10

11

12

13

14

15

Joong-Gun Tul
32 Moves

16

17

18

19

20 - reversed

21- reversed

22 - reversed

23 - reversed

24 - reversed

25 - reversed

26 - reversed

27- reversed

28 - reversed

29 - reversed

30 - reversed

31 - reversed

Joong-Gun Tul 32 Moves

32 - reversed

31 - normal

32 - normal

7. Toi-Gye Tul (37 moves)

Named after the noted scholar, Yi-Hwang, Toi-Gye Tul is a complex tul containing a wide array of complicated techniques. Based heavily on Okinawan kata, Toi-Gye can be seen to contain many of the brutal and dirty techniques common to Okinawan close quarter fighting. But perhaps most distinctive, yet also borrowed from K, is the long sequence of W-shaped blocks and accompanying stamps that make practice of this tul quite a spectator sport.

Kata	Common Moves	Description
Heian Godan	1,2,3,4,5,6	L-stance middle inner forearm block; walking stance low upset fingertip thrust; turn 90^0 to front in closed stance; simultaneous low outer forearm block/back fist (repeat other side)
	7,8	X- fist pressing block; walking stance twin vertical punch
	29,30	Jump landing in X-stance; X-fist pressing block; turn 90^0 and double forearm block in walking stance
Heian Yondan	20,21,22	Head grab; knee kick; turn 180^0 KHGB
Jitte	12, 13, 14, 15, 16, 17, 18	Closed stance hands to hips; W-shaped block and stamp (x6)
Bassai Dai	35, 36	Circular block (x2)

Notes:

1. This pattern is extremely similar to Heian Godan throughout.
2. Move 8 in K is also a high twin arm thrust in walking stance but, unlike TKD, the hands remain crossed.
3. K uses move 12 as a transition move and though (as in TKD) the feet come together and the hands draw across the body in an X-shape, K does not pause in this stance as TKD does.
4. Moves 35 and 36 in Toi-Gye, just like Bassai Dai, are the penultimate moves.
5. Though not a Shotokan kata, an older version of Bassai/Passai created by Matsumura Sokon in the 1800's can be seen to contain about 50% of the techniques of Toi Gye, incuding: circular blocks; low knife hand blocks; sitting stance punches; low block/backfist combination; front kick; double forearm block; and the opening salutation.

Toi-Gye Tul
37 Moves

0

1

2

3

4

5

6

7

8

9

10

11

12

13

14

15

Toi-Gye Tul
37 Moves

16

17

18

19

20

21

22

23 - reversed

24 - reversed

25

26 - reversed

27 - reversed

28

29 - side view

29

30

Toi-Gye Tul
37 Moves

31

32

33

34

35

36

37

8. Hwa-Rang Tul (29 moves)

Hwa-Rang was the first tul to be created. It contains great significance for the new Korean TKD. For example, it contains 29 moves, which is the number of the infantry division where TKD was introduced to the world. The name appeals to a common national identity through capitalising on the legend of the elite Korean Hwa-Rang fighters. Furthermore, invoking the Hwa-Rang legend attempts to, however spuriously, historically legitimise TKD's claims to Korean martial heritage.

Kata	Common Moves	Description
Empi	1,2,3	Sitting stance palm block; sitting stance single punch; sitting stance single punch
Heian Nidan	4, 5, 6	Twin forearm block; upward punch; fixed stance middle punch
Heian Shodan	6,7,8,9	Fixed stance middle punch; vertical stance downward knife hand strike; walking stance obverse punch; 90^0 turn walking stance low block; walking stance middle obverse punch
Taikyoku Sandan	13, 14	Walking stance middle obverse punch (x2)
Heian Nidan	15,16,17	KHGB; 180^0 turn spear hand; KHGB
Heian Sandan	26,27	Closed stance middle inner/low outer forearm block (x2)
Heian Shodan	28, 29	KHGB; 180^0 turn KHGB

Notes:

1. Moves 6,7, 8 and 9: the initial techniques have been modified but the sequence is unmistakably derived from the K version. In TKD, move 6 has been changed from a low block to a fixed stance middle punch. However, the body is still half facing in a long stance and the same arm is extended in both K and TKD. Move 7 uses a knife hand in TKD but a closed fist in K.

2. Move 17 in TKD is 180^0 but in K it is 270^0.

Hwa-Rang Tul
29 Moves

0

1

2

3

4

5

6

7

8

9

10

11

12

12a

13

14

Hwa-Rang Tul
29 Moves

15

16

17

18

19

19a

20

21

22

23

24 - reversed

25

26

27

28

29

태권도

9. Choong-Moo Tul (30 moves)

Choong-Moo, named after the naval genius, Admiral Yi Sun Sin, was the second tul to be designed by Choi, et al. It is very interesting in that it appears to borrow heavily from K kata yet it contains a number of kicks such as the flying side kick and the high turning kick/back kick combination that do not appear in any of the first 13 kata.

Kata	Common Moves	Description
Heian Yondan Kanku Dai/Sho	1,2	Twin knife hand block; high knife hand front strike and other hand to forehead
Heian Yondan	11, 12, 13	Walking stance double front grasp; upward knee kick; 180^0 turn reverse knife hand
Empi	18, 19	U-shaped block; jump and spin landing in KHGB
Heian Godan	20, 21 (22)	Low upset fingertip thrust; pull back into low outer forearm block/back fist

Notes:

1. Move 1 in K holds the front hand lower and the body is angled differently. However, one hand is still raised above the head in both K and TKD. Also interesting is that both Choong-Moo and Heian Yondan have identical first moves.

2. Move 2 is a high strike in Shotokan. However, in some styles of K (for example, Wado Ryu) it is often a lower strike aimed at the kidneys.

3. Move 13 in both K and TKD is a knife hand technique, though it is a KHGB in K and a high reverse knife hand strike in TKD.

4. Flying kick and turning kick/back kick combination represent techniques that are not included in the Okinawan kata. This may be the first real influence of Taekyon on the tuls.

5. Moves 18 and 19 in K have the higher hand with palm upturned to the ceiling. Therefore, this is a grasping block whereas in TKD the palm faces down so it is a U-shaped block.

Although only moves 20 and 21 can be seen in sequence in any of the first 13 Shotokan kata, I have trained moves 20–22 in a Koryu Uchinadi two-person drill. Unfortunately, though they are taken from an ancient kata, their exact derivation remains a mystery to me.

Choong-Moo Tul

30 Moves

0

1

2

3

4

5

6

7

7 side view

8

9 side view

9a

10

11

12

13

Choong-Moo Tul

30 **Moves**

14

15

16

17

18

19

19a

20

20 - reversed

21

21 - reversed

2

22 - reversed

Choong-Moo Tul

30 **Moves**

23

24

24a

25

26

27

28

29

30

Summary of the Results

As can be seen from the comparison above, 61% of templates from the first 9 Chang-Hon Tuls are derived from the first 13 Shotokan Kata (see **Table.2** below). This percentage does not include individual techniques but rather sequences of techniques (two or more) that represent an obvious template. However, though all the tuls contain templates that are present in the kata, the number of templates in each tul varies radically. For example, Won-Hyo Tul is almost an exact copy of the kata Heian Nidan, with 28 of its 28 moves appearing in similar or identical templates within the kata. Conversely, some tuls, such as Joong-Gun and Choong-Moo, contain relatively few kata templates and the templates that they do contain represent a much smaller percentage of the overall techniques contained therein.

Table 2: A summary of the results

Tul	Number of Moves	Number of Moves found in Templates common to Kata/Tul	% of Tul in Kata
Chon-Ji	19	17	89
Dan-Gun	21	14	67
Do-San	24	16	67
Won-Hyo	28	28	100
Yul-Gok	38	18	47
Joong-Gun	32	9	28
Toi-Gye	37	22	59
Hwa-Rang	29	19	66
Choong-Moo	30	9	30
Total	258	152	61

As previously stated, this level of derivation is not surprising because these 13 Shotokan kata are likely to be the kata that General Choi and his technical advisors, mostly Shotokan Karate trained, would have had exposure to. It is not possible to say if the remaining 39% of these tuls are original work or contain templates derived from other sources. Nor is this really important because it is the selection and ordering of templates that makes a kata/tul. Therefore, despite the Chang-Hon series obviously being inspired by the Shotokan kata (especially the Heian series), the Chang-Hon series is still original work (with the exception of Won-Hyo). Furthermore, many of the templates display stylistic variations that appear to modify without sacrificing the defensive integrity of the template.

Differences between the Kata and the Tuls

Perhaps as important as the similarities are the differences between the kata and the tuls. In modifying Karate to create Taekwon-Do, Choi changed many of the hand positions, including the chambers, in an attempt to improve efficiency. Moreover, many of the stances, which were becoming affected by the aesthetic stylism prized by Karate competitions, were shortened or removed altogether, leaving the first 9 tuls with fewer stances than the first 13 kata. This means that the walking stance and the L-stance of Taekwon-Do are used for many more techniques than the original kata required. However, the most important difference is in the progressive introduction of kicks.

As one would expect in a kicking art syllabus, the tuls contain a progression of kicking techniques. These kicks begin as basic in nature, such as a front snap kick (Do–San), and then progress on to more complicated kicks, such as side kick (Won-Hyo) and turning kick (Hwa-Rang). Once the student has shown mastery of the single kicking techniques, combinations are introduced, such as two turning-kicks (Hwa-Rang) or two side kicks (Choong-Moo). In the final coloured belt pattern, Choong-Moo, a number of kicking techniques are introduced, including a turning kick/back kick combination and most notably a flying kick. This approach can be seen to continue up through the black belt tuls with ever more demanding kicks being introduced as the student progresses.

This is a definite departure from the Okinawan kata, which tend to rely on quite basic kicks and appear to use them as a set-up for a hand technique. Furthermore, the incorporation of complicated, and often quite flamboyant, kicks into the tuls gives **some** credence to the influence of Taekyon on their development. However, equally possible is that innovations of kicking techniques (often Korean) inspired by the open competition circuit, gave Choi the impetus to modernise his approach to tuls. Though this is speculation, it is well documented that Choi was enamoured by the athleticism of his young Taekwon-Do pioneers and utilised them in pushing the boundaries of what martial artists could physically achieve. An expression of this could be seen in Choi's obsession with having his demonstrators jump moving cars (Gillis, 2008). Ironically, it is well known that the success of Taekwon-Do kicking on the competition circuit was to influence Karate fighters, with many techniques, such as the reverse turning kick, becoming a standard in Kumite worldwide. However, perhaps the greatest success of Taekwon-Do kicking was that it helped shape the movie career of a young Hong Kong-based movie star called Bruce Lee[4]. It is thought that Lee met Joon Rhee (a respected Taekwon-Do fighter) in 1964 at the Long Beach Karate championships. They were said to swap techniques, with Rhee teaching Lee the side kick.

Discussion

What is clear from looking at this comparison is that there are far too many similarities to be attributed to mere coincidence. In fact, it is obvious, even to the uninitiated, that all of the Chang-Hon Tuls are, to a lesser or major degree, influenced by the kata that Choi and his technical advisors would have learnt whilst studying Karate. However, though the level of similarity is alarming in some tuls (for example, Won-Hyo), it is varied enough in others to avoid a charge of plagiarism and to represent original work in the choreography necessary for such compilation. After all, this is exactly what Itosu achieved when distilling older kata such as Jion and Kanku-Dai into his modernised Heian series.

It is possible to claim that the work of both Choi and Itosu was original because the templates inherited from Chinese Hsing (kata) were common property. The templates represent set fighting sequences and therefore it is highly probable that the same templates would be contained in any fighting system that is governed by similar strategic principles. Indeed, most of the kata contained in Shotokan Karate (excluding the Heian series) are of Chinese origin and therefore most of Shotokan's fighting templates were inherited from the Chinese Hsing present in the Kung Fu styles that the Okinawans were exposed to (predominantly White Crane and Monk Fist). Furthermore, some of the kata represent Okinawan versions of Chinese Hsing yet others are the work of masters from either the Naha, Shuri or Tomari districts of Okinawa where these kata would have been created and taught in complete secrecy. Therefore, there is much stylistic variation within the kata themselves.

The kata contain many different ways of doing the same thing, as each kata designer would put their individual take on things. It may be argued that by designing his own kata/tuls, Choi has attempted to reduce the variation by imposing a wholly Korean style on all the tuls. Though this approach does not address the rich cultural and historical heritage that the kata offer, it does offer consistency, which in turn reduces confusion and ambiguity; all improvements that a student would find beneficial.

What the comparison offers

One benefit of the comparison is that we are able to begin to see the tuls at the level of the template and not at the level of the constituent parts, i.e. the techniques. Such an approach is akin to looking at a working clock, rather than being given a collection of lifeless cogs and springs that confound more than enlighten. By comparing the kata and the tuls, we are able to recognise, as were Choi, et al., where these sequences begin and end. By doing so, it is possible to begin to interpret, through 'bunkai', the 'oyo' or applications of the templates in terms that transcend mere block, kick and punch. By recognising the defensive strategies inherent in the precursor styles of Kung Fu, such as grappling, throwing and clinch work, as well as the percussive techniques which form the basis of modern Karate and Taekwon-Do, we are able to see that originally Karate was developed as a complete fighting system covering all distances and levels of aggression. Furthermore, by looking at the adaptations that Choi, et al. made to many of these templates, it is clear that Choi had both a working knowledge of kata applications and enough understanding of the defensive principles therein to make efficient and effective changes to the original templates. Unfortunately, for historical reasons, including the deliberate occlusion of dangerous techniques in Karate kata to permit their widespread dissemination, nearly all of the original kata applications have been lost or misinterpreted. This situation has been even more exacerbated in Taekwon-Do, with many respected senior grades, including original pioneers such as Grandmaster Kong stating openly that there is no interpretation to the tuls other than that offered by General Choi. This has led to a dogma within ITF Taekwon-Do that has blinkered its practitioners, making even the mere suggestion of 'alternative' or 'hidden applications' heretical. Such a climate of fear is not only unproductive but also undermines the whole defensive capability of the art, as most of the 'surface level' applications of techniques offered by the ITF simply do not work in practice and may even endanger a student who is foolish enough to rely on them in combat. Furthermore, it begs the question of why we need hundreds of different techniques to block a straight punch. As has been shown through the adaptations that Choi made to many templates, he understood fully that the kata were operating on a paradigm that was far more complex than the block, kick and punch interpretations that the ITF currently offers.

There may be many reasons why Choi decided to keep the true applications secret but we will never know for sure. It may be that:

1. He believed that the civilian population had no real need of such dangerous techniques and that teaching them openly may restrict the spread of such an international art.

2. He had planned to reveal the true applications to senior grades when he felt he could trust them. This may be difficult to imagine now but in the days before DVDs and the internet it would have been much easier to keep a secret.

3. Choi witnessed the successful spread of Karate and decided to base his expansion on that model, including the removal of applications.

4. As Taekwon-Do took seed in the military, it became necessary to simplify the syllabus so that its teaching could be achieved in basic training (typically five weeks). As mastery of Taekwon-Do's tul applications would take decades, its inclusion in basic training would seem

counterproductive. Interestingly, this is one of the reasons why the previously impressed Japanese Imperial Army did not offer Karate training to its recruits.

5. He did not in fact know most of them. This is highly likely because, according to Motobu, Choki Choi's major influence, Funakoshi Gichin, did not know them to pass on either.

Unfortunately, we will never truly know the reasons for the exclusion of realistic applications from Taekwon-Do instruction because that secret has gone to the grave with Choi. All that is certain is that, because many of the templates outdate Choi by centuries, perhaps students should be encouraged to look beyond the surface level interpretation of the applications offered by Choi and the ITF. After all, if there are better explanations that predate Choi, then they belong to Taekwon-Do just as much as Choi's explanations.

Implications

It should be said that in the post-war years (civil as well as World War II) the hatred of the Japanese by the Koreans was completely understandable. However, most of us who practise Taekwon-Do are neither Korean nor of sufficient age to bear a grudge against the Imperial Japanese Army. Therefore, it is not disloyal or unpatriotic to recognise the dominant role in the ancestry of our martial art that Karate plays. Neither does it weaken our art to admit that it was derived from Karate. After all, Taekwon-Do is a modern art form and the true genius of Choi was that he took an ancient art and modernised it for the 20th century. Furthermore, it is only when we are not ashamed of our links to Karate that we are able to benefit from the rich history and resources available to Karate practitioners.

Some of the many resources that may help unravel the riddle that is kata (tuls) are:

1. **The Bubishi:** an ancient text passed from master to student, which contains much information on pressure points and their effects as well as drawings and explanations of defensive strategies against aggressors. This historical document, Chinese in origin, represented one of Karate's best kept secrets until very recently.

2. **Lost concepts:** knowledge of the concepts that were essential study in ancient Kung Fu and Toudi is vital when attempting to understand the kata/tul. Though many of these concepts have all but disappeared from modern Karate and Taekwon-Do, there are at least Japanese names for these concepts; even if their translations never made it into Taekwon-Do. Examples of these concepts are:

- **Hikite:** a pulling hand used to control or off balance an opponent. This is often the reason why a hand returns to the belt during a kata technique.

- **Bunkai:** the study of kata applications.
- **Oyo:** the application of a kata technique, coming as a result of bunkai study.
- **Henka:** a variation on an application. After doing bunkai to find an oyo, we may then ponder what adaptations could and would be necessary depending on changes in responses or circumstances and how could these variations be achieved.
- **Muchimi:** this is the controlling of limbs without grabbing or holding. It is very similar to the Chinese concepts of sticking hands and trapping.
- **Kyusho Juitsu:** pressure point manipulation.
- **Qinna (Chin-Na):** this is the Chinese Kung Fu concept of joint manipulation. It involves attacking the joints, separating: muscle from bone; bone from bone; tendons from bones; and pain compliance. This is such a fundamental part of White Crane Kung Fu strategy that it would make up a large part of any Chinese-influenced kata. The Japanese term for this is 'Kansetsu-Waza'.

3. **Tales of the old masters:** writings and stories of old Karate masters and pioneers such as Itosu and Mabuni still exist and can provide students with a real feeling of historical context through which to understand the development of Karate and thus Taekwon-Do.
4. **Funakoshi's books:** Funakoshi left many works, including some early texts that both illustrate and explain many of the techniques which are now readily mislabelled. As a pioneer of Karate, Funakoshi saw the rapid change his art underwent and commented upon this in his literature.
5. **Bunkai debunkers:** currently, there is some outstanding bunkai work being done by highly respected martial artists such as Patrick McCarthy and Iain Abernethy. These Karate scholars are attempting to revive many of the original practices of Karate in an attempt to breathe life once more into kata. Because Taekwon-Do shares many templates with Karate, the work of these individuals is highly relevant to any Taekwon-Do student who may wish to make the tuls work in real life.

To reiterate, as practitioners of traditional martial arts (TMA), we should neither fear our history nor our ancestry. In an era which is increasingly seeing TMA edged aside by the new boys of 'reality-based martial arts' and mixed martial arts (MMA), we should embrace what it is that makes us unique. As students of a fighting system, a moral code and a history are all that really set us apart from MMA fighters. Denial of either of these treasures weakens us and may make the future of TMA uncertain. As the old saying goes: "How can you know where you're going if you don't know where you've been?"

태권도

태권도

태권도

Chapter 2: Blocking:
The most confused and confusing part of Taekwon-Do

Famously, and rather accidently in the spirit of self-parody, neoconservative and utter black-heart, US Secretary of State Donald Rumsfeld said to much hilarity and derision in reference to the situation in Iraq/Afghanistan: "There are known knowns and known unknowns and unknown unknowns". Whilst it is undeniable that are more eloquent turns of phrase, this principle remains sound.

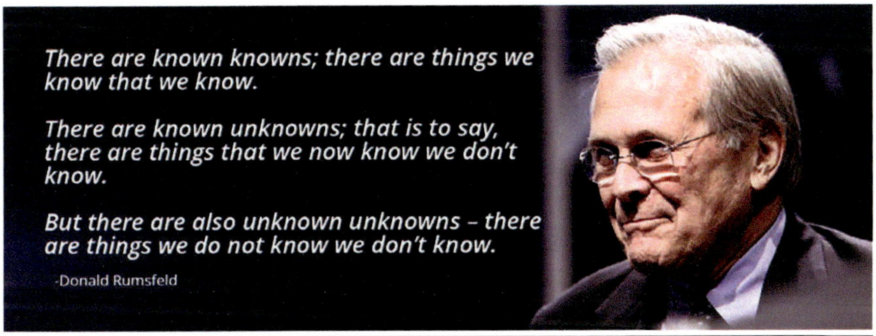

Figure 10: Donald Rumsfeld's "Known Knowns"

There are:

1. things we know are within our knowledge base;
2. things we recognise are beyond our current knowledge or understanding; and
3. things we are not aware of existing **and thus do not know about**.

This tryptic of empiricisms can be said to accurately describe the knowledge of most Taekwon-Do students and instructors (henceforth TKDers). Whilst occupying one or all of these positions is not a problem, the danger comes when we do not recognise the existence of things that fall into the last of the statements above. For, if we are to offer guidance and opinions based on the premise that we are in total possession of the facts, yet there are factors that exist that we are not aware of, then it is likely that we are 'talking out of our hat'. In many fields of enterprise and education, claiming to be an authority on something whilst clearly not fully understanding your subject will result in an immediate challenge to the legitimacy of such claims; however, not in the world of TMA. Illegitimate claims to be an authority are rarely checked in TMA. This is mainly down to the culture of deference and filial piety perpetuated by the dominant hierarchical structure of TMA originating in the East. This structure is referred to as the Sempai-Kohai system. In this top-down relationship, the questioning of authority is seen as a breach of protocol and an act of disloyalty. Whilst Confucian- based societies like China, Korea and Japan are more conformable with this dogmatic approach to knowledge conservation, it is totally at odds with the type of critical thought prevalent in the Western paradigm of post-enlightenment thinking, where questioning givens is seen as the basis of education and development. Nevertheless, TMA in the West has for so long adopted the Sempai-Kohai whilst foolishly believing that it prevents them from critically evaluating the claims made by instructors and literature within the purview of their particular martial art. Within Taekwon-Do, such dogma and a fear of being controversial has prevented us as a community from tackling the thorny issue of what are and how to use the Chang-Hon Tuls (the patterns or kata). To effectively study the tuls and uncover their applications, TKDers must admit that:

Figure 11: Foot Fist Way - Unchecked Authority

- most of our patterns are derived from older Karate kata (see previous chapter);
- we do not know what the applications for these patterns are; and
- it is as least **possible** that those who taught us did not know the applications either.

In my capacity as a Taekwon-Do instructor, I have travelled the world meeting martial artists and I have never met anyone who knows what the applications for the Chang-Hon Tuls are. This includes senior masters and grand masters.

Though the study of kata applications, referred to as bunkai, is of growing popularity and is emerging as a movement that is challenging the orthodoxy in modern Karate, there is no major culture of bunkai that is encouraged in Taekwon-Do. Yes, there are individuals and outrider groups, but the *Encyclopaedia* (both the 15-volume set and condensed versions) published by General Choi in 1983, and updated in 1999 (see Figure.12), discourages bunkai because it gives the student all the applications. Unfortunately, all these applications are against a kick or a straight punch and so do not cover the wide variety of attacks one would need for good 'self-defence'. Furthermore, the explanations we were given by the General were inaccurate, incomplete or utterly ludicrous. That is not to say that the General, though flawed, was not a great man. He was. He achieved great things and created a beautiful and inclusive art whose popularity is worldwide. He unified, although briefly, the disparate kwans in a bid to forge a martial art with a cultural identity that was no longer beholden to the colonial past of the hated Japanese occupiers. But he did not provide us with:

- a plausible explanation of the techniques contained in the patterns;
- a method of safely training these techniques with a partner; and
- a team of well-trained instructors who understood and could teach the applications of the patterns.

Figure 12: Choi's Encyclopaedia

Instead, we are left with a book (the *Encyclopaedia*) that perpetuates the poor understanding of the applications that we inherited from the Japanese, who had lost the knowledge of their kata long before 1955. Like Karate, Taekwon-Do has replaced function with form. If we don't understand the applications of the patterns then we must concentrate on them 'looking good'. After all, we need to teach something. And so 'authorities' on the Taekwon-Do patterns have become those who know what a pattern should look like rather that what it was for or what applications it contains. Though sad, such a situation is not terrible because the vast majority of TKDers do not study patterns for their utility but rather for their aesthetic qualities and/or 'as a method of improving one's character' (an ethos consistent with the 'Tao' or 'Do' suffix associated with these arts). However, as Rumsfeld would point out, we need to be wary of the 'unknown knowns'. Indeed, problems occur when such authorities claim to know the applications of the patterns when they clearly don't and thus discredit themselves and our art. Nowhere is this more apparent than in the common misunderstanding of the multitude of weird and wonderful blocks contained within the art (see Figure.13).

The problems with 'traditional' blocking

Though placing a limb in front of an attack to prevent damage is a necessary part of any martial art, the way in which Taekwon-Do perceives and teaches blocking makes little sense. Some of the many problems of Taekwon-Do's approach to blocking are that:

- The blocks don't work in the way we were shown them because engagement distances are unrealistic.
- The word 'block' is a misnomer and sets up a false characterisation of blocking and a method of meeting force with force.
- If everything is a block, a kick or a punch, where are the joint locks and strangulations?
- There is no capitalising on the body's natural defence mechanisms, for example, the flinch.
- There are too many blocks and thus it will be difficult to select 'the correct one' under pressure.
- There is no satisfactory explanation for why we need a chamber before blocking.

We shall therefore limit ourselves to addressing these issues. Much of what follows has been men-

Figure.13 : Unrealistic ideas of violence

tioned elsewhere by others who share these sentiments. However, the solutions as perceived by this author are derived from his study and teaching of old school Karate and the associated practices and strategies that have been lost or shunned by modern Karate.

Set sparring: unrealistic engagement distances

The idea of what a block is comes from set sparring. This is when and only when many of these blocks work. The drill is usually predicated on the model of:

1. one person (the attacker) goes back into a long walking stance with a low block;
2. the other person stands in chumbi, hands by the belt apparently ready;
3. the attacker and defender both loudly affirm that they are ready;
4. the attacker executes an attack, usually a middle obverse punch whilst stepping forward; and
5. the defender steps back and blocks and thus avoids being defeated.

Figure.14 : A typical set sparring routine with its obvious lack of realism

In this scenario, the defence, i.e. the block, is successful because the conditions are perfect for it to succeed. Namely:

- the engagement distance is unrealistic;
- the attacker knows in advance what is going to happen;
- the attacker usually warns the defender he/she is coming, either with a shout or a big sine wave; and
- the defender has so much time to react that he/she can even start with hands down; not protecting in a guard or 'fence' but rather just hanging in chumbi.

The origins of set sparring

According to world kata authority, Patrick McCarthy (2018), the drill is a ritual based on the Japanese tradition of Kendo/Iaido and was bequeathed to us from a modern Japanese understanding of Karate. Owing to its origin in Kendo/Iaido, set sparring is based on the 'kill with a single blow' principle of sword fighting (ikken-hissatsu). This principle was to be erroneously applied to Karate techniques and thus become part of Karate and later Taekwon-Do mythology. Furthermore, McCarthy tells us that, prior to the introduction of Okinawan Karate to the Japanese mainland in the 1920s, this ritual did not exist in Okinawa in this form. This is important because it is often viewed by TKDers as a traditional method of learning to defend oneself. The use of the term 'traditional' is often to elevate something to the level of sacrosanct and thus render it beyond question. The term is also frequently used as an explanation for something when an adequate expository response is unknown. However, a lack of set sparring in pre-war Okinawan Karate tells us that it was not viewed by the originators of the art as a suitable method of drilling the techniques contained within the kata. Furthermore, McCarthy also reveals that the early developers of set sparring did not themselves know applications for the blocks. Thus, the techniques of set sparring were retro-fitted applications based on a flawed understanding of the nature of 'blocks'.

Figure 15: Group training in Okinawa's public school system (circa 1937)

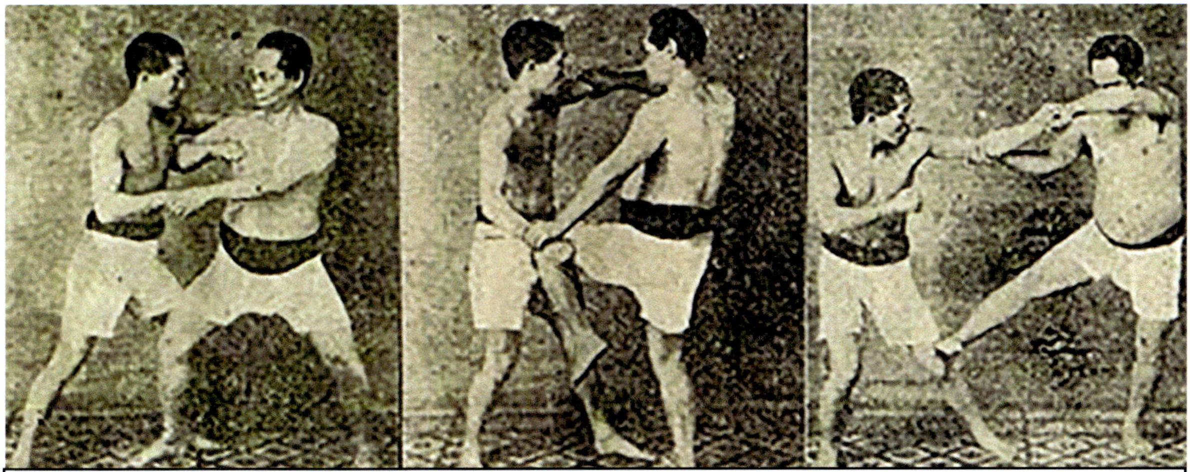

Figure 16: Choki Motobu: Karate pioneer; street fighter; and critic of Funakoshi

The loss of the original applications and the creation of new erroneous ones

Figure 17: Funakoshi Gichin Father of Modern Karate

One of the main reasons for the loss of knowledge that led to blocks being incorrectly interpreted was the introduction of Karate to the Okinawa school system in 1901 (OIG, 2018). On its introduction, the main method of instruction became kata and line work or kihon – another modern invention (see Figure.15). The teaching of applications was neither necessary nor advisable when educating children to become healthy conformist recruits for the expanding Japanese war machine; a goal openly stated by Ankoh Itosu (the teacher of Funakoshi), in his *10 Precepts of Karate.* Many of the early Japanese Karate instructors were products of this system and did not themselves understand the applications of the kata. Furthermore, the vast majority of instructors had no real-world experience of violence and therefore could not pressure test the flawed kata applications. Funakoshi himself (see Figure.17), the founder of Shotokan Karate (a precursor to Taekwon-Do and by far the most popular form of modern Karate) was publicly ridiculed by Karate master and famed street fighter Motobu Choki (see Figure.16) for his poor understanding of kata applications. Motobu likened Funakoshi to a particular Okinawan stringed instrument (shamisen), saying he made a lovely sound but was ultimately hollow inside (McCarthy, n.d.).

Owing to the deferential and conformist nature of Japanese society and the Sempai-Kohai product of it, once such false interpretations of kata applications had been established by seniors, they could not be questioned by juniors; a situation inherited by Western dojos/dojangs and perpetuated to this day.

Problems with set sparring

Figure 18: A serious lack of realism

As a method of training for self-defence, set sparring it is at best risible and at its worse dangerously irresponsible. Firstly, it is unrealistic. Personally, I would suggest walking away from any potential attacker the minute they take a long walking stance and low block. Ask any door supervisor or police officer and they will tell you how rare it is to be attacked in this way and from such a distance (see Figure.18). Violent attacks are often sudden and overwhelming. Attackers often use stealth or distraction to breach gaps and may even attack you from behind or from hiding. Stepping backwards and declaring your intent is the behaviour of someone who is likely trying to avoid violence, but gives the appearance of assertive alpha male social behaviour (Miller, 2011).

The block only works because the conditions are perfect for it to succeed. If you change any of the conditions – vary the attack, start without any warning, hit the defender from up close or from behind – then the block won't work anymore. Of course, the flip side to this is when conditions are so perfect for defence anything works. Try it! Start by defending with a middle block, then use a finger, a newspaper, your shoe, a cabbage, your belly. Pretty much anything will work.

Lastly, like many wholly Japanese pursuits, the ritual of set sparring is more important than the utility of the exercise. That is to say, owing to the Japanese perspective on pursuing perfection as a pursuit in itself in all walks of life, set sparring has become much more about 'doing it right' than 'how does it help?'. This can be seen by analysing what makes good set sparring within Taekwon-Do, where height of block, length of stance, correct foot positions and graceful sine wave have become more important criteria than self-protection.

So, to summarise this discussion on set sparring:

- It is **not** a traditional method of training the techniques contained within the patterns.
- It uses blocks in a retro-fitted interpretation that is modern and based on a flawed under standing of the nature of violence.
- It is unrealistic in its attack patterns and distances and thus ineffective for self-defence.
- It is an overly ritualised practice where the focus is on form over function.

How does this help us?

- Once we establish the futility of training under such conditions. we can begin to see beyond the dogma and find more appropriate methods of training (an area that will be covered later).
- Once we begin to recognise the nature of violence. we can better prepare for it and thus select techniques, blocks included, that work under such conditions.
- Once we begin to take these steps. we can begin to better understand our own art.

The erroneousness of blocking as force meets force

It has been widely documented elsewhere that the term 'block' in Karate does not in fact translate as block but rather means to receive. This may seem like a slight distinction until you apply it to other non-martial arts contexts, for example, traffic, post, football, as follows:

Figure 19: The rising block commonly used to jam an arm; control an opponent; or as a choke

- **Traffic**: block creates a jam; to receive creates continuous flow or good parking
- **Post**: block letterbox remains closed and impenetrable; received post is delivered
- **Football**: block means to prevent a goal, pass or movement; receive means to facilitate another action

What can be seen by analysing these examples is that they all contain linguistic commonalities. Namely, that blocking tends to stop the movement of something whereas receiving tends to permit movement, which results in a possibility of continuation. To block something implies a use of force to impede movement whereas to receive means to permit movement and thus the consequences become possibilities. The translation of the Japanese word 'uke' is of particular relevance to Taekwon-Do as Taekwon-Do inherited most of its terms from Shotokan Karate. This is why the term 'makgi', meaning block, is so widely used. That is not to say that Karate and thus Taekwon-Do does not contain blocks in the traditional sense. It does!

There are blocks and there are other things called blocks

All fighting systems include a method of stopping a blow to the body or to the head simply by raising your arms or legs to impede the connection of the attack with the target. At times, it is all one can do to prevent injury, especially if an attack is unexpected and furious (as most violence is). However, such blocking is more instinctive than learnt and relies heavily on the body's inbuilt flinch reaction (a subject that will be covered later). Many revisionists, so-called bunkai 'experts', have mistakenly stated that there are no blocks in Karate/Taekwon-Do. Unfortunately for them, there are. The problem is identifying which techniques mistakenly labelled makgi are blocks and which are in fact something else. The confusion is further compounded by the fact that, though the body may have limited movement, each movement can have a multitude of applications depending on the context. A good example of this is a rising block, which is referred to in grappling arts as a sliding collar choke or a sliding lapel choke, but it is also used as: a method of clearing an arm and exposing a floating rib target; a strike to the jaw; a method of destroying a joint; and a method of controlling an opponent against a wall (see Figure.19). In truth, the applications may vary but the principles required to use the body to apply upward force remain consistent in every good application.

Figure 20: A Thai block with the shin used to block kicks

Machismo and blocking

Another element that compounds our misunderstanding is the hard blocking practices of Shotokan. Shotokan is famous for its powerful straight-line attacks and blocks. This is obviously a consequence of young men spurring each other on to go faster and harder. However, as already alluded to, this practice is based on a poor representation of the nature of violence and a misinterpretation of the kata techniques. The desire to inflict damage on an opponent by use of hard blocking is laudable. However, if the blocks were not intended to be used in their current 'traditional applications' then increasing the speed and power of their execution is going to add little to their efficacy. In most full contact fighting sports, such as Muay Thai or MMA, you never see anyone defend against a front kick or a roundhouse with a low block in this manner in open sparring. The reasons for this become apparent when you try it. The tibia is very heavy and dense and the radius or ulna bones of the wrist are much lighter and weaker. Attempting to stop a fast-moving tibia with a wrist in a force meets force manner is bound to end in injury to the blocker. Full contact fighters and most TKDers instinctively know this and therefore wise ones **never** try to do so. In such a situation, the harder you strike the tibia the greater the risk of injury to the arm. Such a probability of injury is why full contact kicking arts such as Muay Thai employ a conditioned tibia to block a kick (see Figure.20). However, 'blocking a kick' with a wrist or hand using force meeting force is still the prevalent application of a low block in TKD.

Low block as a redirect

Interestingly, the low block in Karate (Gedan Barai) is also referred to as a low 'sweeping block'. Used in a sweeping motion, it can be easily employed to redirect the force of a straight-line kick, rather than stop it. When redirecting force, the defender uses the attacker's speed and power against them in order to create imbalance or to worsen the attacker's position and thereby facilitate a better target for counter attack. This is the whole principle of Aikido (an art derived from Ju Jitsu). To see the benefits of such an approach, one need only think of the bullfighter and his/her ability to deal with the hugely powerful charges of half a ton of enraged bull (see Figure.21). Meeting force with force in such circumstances would predictably result in the injury or perhaps death of the matador. Redirecting the charge of the bull requires little physical force from the matador and capitalises on the immense strength and speed of the bull.

Figure 21: Classic redirection of force

Figure 22: Low block as an arm bar

Redirecting kicks is best applied to straight-line attacks such as a side kick or a front kick. If indeed such a technique were effective, we would expect to see it in some form in both Taekwon-Do sparring and full contact arts, which employs many straight-line kicking techniques. Consistently, with this analysis, redirecting of kicks with the forearm is very much an established response to straight-line techniques common in Taekwon-Do sparring. Furthermore, redirecting kicks in an attempt to catch them is also a common response to all manner of front kicks used in MMA.

The low block as a joint attack

As previously mentioned, the applications for a technique are determined by the context, i.e. is the guy kicking you, punching you or grabbing you? In many grappling-based arts, the 'low block' is in fact used as a method of locking and pressuring the elbow joint of an opponent (an application we will cover later). When inspected closely, it is apparent that the mechanics of the low block and the arm bar joint lock are identical (see Figure.22). The different applications result from the need to respond to the differing contexts, i.e. is someone kicking you, punching you or grabbing you? This is a common occurrence and a principle worth keeping in mind when attempting to decipher the code of the Chang-Hon Tuls. It is only when we view applications in the limited terms of block-kick-punch that we limit our perspective and therefore blinker ourselves to 'everything' loosely belonging to one of those three categories. The desire to block everything in the 'meet force with force' perspective came as a direct result of Karate becoming a block-kick-punch art; a situation that we will discuss next.

So, to summarise:

- The term 'block' is a misinterpretation of the Japanese term 'uke' and a better translation would be 'to receive'.
- Taekwon-Do patterns do contain true blocks, but fewer than we currently believe.
- The body makes limited movements but the applications of such movements can be infinite.
- Context determines application, i.e. are you being kicked, punched or grabbed?
- Blocks that employ force against force can result in injury to the blocker and therefore redirection is preferable.

If everything is a block a kick or a punch where are the joint locks, throws and strangulations?

All complete martial art systems include methods of defending and attacking at all ranges. These systems incorporate techniques and counters against the types of attacks the originator of that system deemed most likely to be encountered. Some systems are weapons based, for example, Escrima and Kali, whilst others are not, for example, Karate and Taekwon-Do (though Kobudo was very much an auxiliary part of pre-war Karate). However, for a weaponless system to call itself complete it must contain some knowledge of:

- striking with hands and other parts of the body;
- kicking;
- air deprivation, i.e. choking and strangulations;
- rudimentary ground fighting;
- balance displacement;
- vulnerable areas;
- seizing and controlling: manipulation of joints, cavities and connective tissue; and
- defences/escapes from all of the above.

As can be seen from a cursory look at most modern systems, they are incomplete. This is due to two main reasons:

1. Their need to specialise in order to distinguish themselves from other arts.
2. The development of their rule-bound sporting form.

Many great arts such as boxing, Judo/BJJ (formally Ju-Jitsu) and Karate used to be complete and contain all of the above elements to a greater or lesser degree. However, all the aforementioned underwent modernisation and became specialists. All the great founders of modern Karate, for example, Funakoshi Gichin, Mabuni Kenwa and Miyagi Chojan, have at some point referred in their writings to the differences between modern Karate and that which they studied in Okinawa. All have stated that Karate used to contain throws, joint locks and strangulation. However, as has been covered elsewhere, Karate underwent a rapid process of modernisation during its introduction to Japan and the university system in the 1920s. To receive ratification from Japan's national martial arts authority (Butokukai) and be recognised as a budo, it had to:

- systematise;
- adopt a ranking belt system;
- create uniforms;
- develop a sport side so that young men could test their skills in relative safety; and
- distinguish itself from other arts in the budo tradition.

Thus, Karate became a block-kick-punch art; an area previously unexploited by other budo arts such as Kendo, Judo and Sumo. It was necessary for Karate to specialise in these techniques because Judo provided ground fighting, balance displacement and air deprivation and Kendo/Iaido provided the weapons. Therefore, it was obvious that, to fit in, Karate would have to adopt the blocking, kicking and punching left over. Once established, this quickly became the perspective through which the lost kata applications became understood and deciphered. Such unrealistic interpretations of kata were further bolstered by the development of a long-range kick, punch and block sport form, which ultimately became the focus of many Karateka and guaranteed the existence of Karate until today.

Unfortunately, the kata predated the modernisation of Karate and they were developed when Karate was taught as a complete system. It has been widely documented that Okinawan Karate was heavily influenced by Chinese Kung Fu and that the styles most influential on the development of the kata were Monk-Fist Boxing and White Crane (Cohen, 2018). It is a fact that both these styles were complete arts and incorporated all of the elements listed above. Not only that but they placed great emphasis on Chin-Na (also known as Qin Na).

Chin-Na: The basis of all kata and tuls

Chin-Na is a method of seizing and controlling an opponent through manipulating pressure points, cavities, joints and air/blood deprivation. It is a skilled practice that was used readily by law enforcement officers in China and Okinawa to control their prisoners. Examination of Chin-Na practices reveals a plethora of kata applications and postures. However, it is employed at close quarters. Therefore, the distance required to use it differs greatly from the long range necessary to block, kick and punch in the way promoted by modern Karate. This is an important point because the modern interpretations of classical kata have labelled nearly all techniques as a block, a kick or a punch. Therefore, this leads one to ask the question: "If everything is a block a kick or a punch, where are the wrist locks, arm bars, takedowns, throws, chokes, strangulations and cavity seizing so characteristic of Chin-Na?" The answer is obvious: they are all there and are just erroneously labelled as blocks or punches.

If we are to recognise these techniques for what they really are, then we need to first acquire knowledge of a grappling art such as Chin-Na or classical Ju-Jitsu, where we can learn the techniques in isolation and then attempt to locate them in the classical kata. A common mistake that many TKDers make when trying to interpret the tuls is that they use their Taekwon-Do knowledge to do so. Unfortunately, unless one's instructor comes from a grappling background and has passed on these techniques, then it is highly unlikely that one's Taekwon-Do will reflect the amount of grappling knowledge required to decipher the tuls. Therefore, it will be necessary to study another art or meet someone who has.

Balance displacement

Balance displacement is another fundamental pillar of White Crane Kung Fu, Monk Fist Boxing and

Figure 23: Funakoshi Gichin demonstrating one of the 9 throws included in his 1935 book

all complete arts. Balance displacement is a method of removing an opponent's ability to strike effectively. This concept is reflected in techniques that are designed to change the position of an attacker from vertical to horizontal. It therefore encompasses throws, takedowns, sweeps and any action that will compromise the balance of the attacker. It is a great strategy in self-defence. After all, when an attacker is falling, they are not striking, and, when they are thinking about falling, they are not concentrating on striking. Unfortunately, balance displacement has fallen out of favour with Taekwon-Do and modern Karate. This is mainly due to a lack of mats, expertise, time, perceived relevance and the need for Karate historically to distinguish itself from Judo. Nowhere in his explanation of the applications of the tuls does the General mention balance displacement.

Modern Karate has a similar attitude to balance displacement and indeed it is often remarked by less informed instructors that Karate has no throws. This is ill-informed nonsense and the writings of all the Karate pioneers talk about throws. Indeed, Funakoshi was known to teach nine throws (see Figure.23) and these appeared in his early work (Funakoshi, 1935), though they mysteriously disappeared in the later reprints (Funakoshi, 1973). Even General Choi recognised the need to address balance displacement and dedicated space to it in his 1965 book as well as including it in both his condensed encyclopaedia and the extended version. So why is there no balance displacement in the patterns? **Well there is!** Again, they are just mislabelled as blocks or strikes. If one examines a throwing art like Judo, one will see many of the set-up positions necessary for throws and takedowns. Similarly, many of the stances, for example, the low stance and the X-stance, can be effectively used to drop the weight of the defender in order to further manipulate a fallen attacker (see Figure.24).

Figure 24: Balance displacement and ground control

Balance displacement is a subject that requires much more space and will therefore be further discussed in a later chapter. However, it is sufficient here to say that the Chang-Hon Tuls contain many methods of taking down an opponent and disrupting their balance. Though these techniques are erroneously labelled as blocks or strikes, by looking at throwing arts (and old Karate manuals such as the Bubishi) we can see how frequently they appear in our patterns.

Using the body's natural defence mechanisms: the flinch

The body contains natural pre-programmed responses to certain stimuli. These may differ greatly or not at all from individual to individual but, when faced with a surprise or an imminent pain, most of us flinch. The flinch is commonly a method of throwing one's hands up to protect oneself whilst drawing back the head from the stimuli (see Figure.25). It occurs very quickly. The strength of its response time is that it occurs without the need for conscious thought. Therefore, it is faster than any response that requires conscious thought and enacting of a decision-making process. This can be best described by looking at the concept of the 'OODA' loop (see Figure.26). This is a concept that American firearms trainers readily use to train recruits (Miller, 2011). It shows how responses to violent encounters often require a four-stage process, with the ability to 'take action' often being dependent on the sequential completion of the other three stages of 'observe, orient and decide' **first.** The issue with this process is that quite often the unpredictable nature of violence forces the victim into a state of disorientation and each subsequent blow may short cut the loop. This means that the victim never gets out of the two initial stages of 'observe and orient' and thus is never able to respond by formulating a plan and acting upon it. Unconscious actions do not conform to the four-stage loop and therefore are not hampered by the sequential interdependency of all the stages.

Figure 25: The flinch position

While it is possible via purposeful and repetitive training (operon) to train something to become a flinch, it is questionable whether one could or should attempt to train more than one flinch response to the same type of stimuli, for example, a straight punch. After all, selecting from options requires conscious thought, and conscious thought slows things down. If our objective is to limit the need for a conscious decision-making process, then learning a vast array of supposed blocks that we are told are designed to do the same thing is unwise. It is known that, having to select an appropriate response under

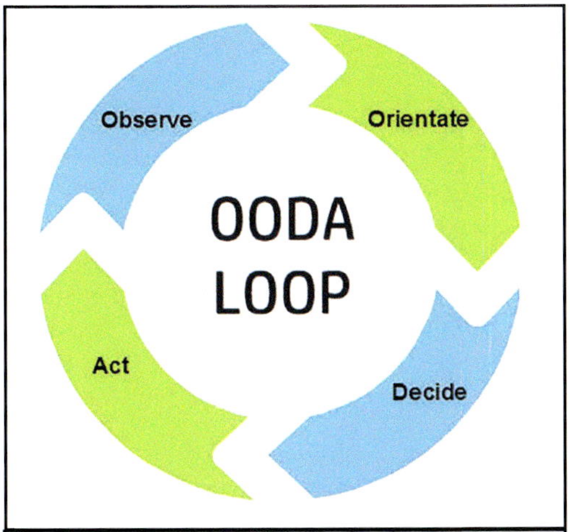

Figure 26: The OODA loop

pressure when the options are multitude is likely to require too much conscious discrimination, either qualifying or disqualifying options until the best one is selected. Under pressure, and particularly under the type of pressure encountered in violence, this can result in a 'logjam', i.e. the decision cannot be made fast enough due to the distraction of too many options and therefore no decision is made in time (Thompson, 1997).

A simple remedy to this is to have **one** well-trained response, as alluded to above, trained to a flinch-like response rate. Another option is to have blocks that are based on the same shape as the average flinch response. Unfortunately, due to stylistic reasons, most arts (Taekwon-Do included) have modified their blocking for aesthetic reasons. Therefore, often the blocks take on a quality that was not there when they were first conceived. Two good examples of this are middle block and the KHGB. These will be discussed next when we focus on the thorny issue of the chamber position. However, even a cursory glance at a Taekwon-Do manual such as the *Encylopaedia* will tell you that there are scores of supposed blocks, weird and wonderful, with which to deal with either a kick or a straight punch. Though it is good to have some variety in a system, selecting from such a plethora of options is bound to be problematic under pressure. Luckily for TKDers, when properly understood through the perspective of old school Karate, the main Taekwon-Do blocks can be seen to utilise the body's inbuilt flinch response, and indeed this will now be shown to be the purpose of the mystical 'chamber'.

The chamber: why and what?

The biggest problem with 'traditional blocking' and the poor explanations that accompany it is the chamber.

> *"There is no real explanation in any of the Taekwon-Do material why we need both hands to block with."*

Sergeant Rory Miller once said: "If you need both hands to block, then you're in the wrong fight" (Miller, 2012). According to this expert on violence, when fighting at close range you need to be

Figure 27: Why current explanations of the chamber don't hold water

engaged in at least one of the following:

- Doing damage.
- Improving your position.
- Worsening your opponent's position.
- Avoiding damage. (Miller, 2012)

These are sound principles for fighting. The problem with the chamber position in its Taekwon-Do traditional sense is that it flouts these principles. Let us take for example the middle block. This is commonly employed against a straight punch to the mid-section. The action is as follows:

1. The attacker throws a straight punch.
2. The defender moves his/her hands away from the punch.
3. The defender's wrists make a cross shape (chamber).
4. The defender moves his/her cross back towards the punch whilst stepping forward.
5. The lower hand sweeps up, redirecting the punch using the power of the core and the mo-

mentum of the defender's step while the other (reaction) hand returns to the hip.

In such a defensive sequence the chamber makes no sense. Why when the punch is thrown does the defender cross his/her hands in the chamber position before meeting the punch with a sweeping forearm? What is unusual about this action is that, rather than simply moving towards the attacking object as quickly as possible and thus impeding its action (the principle of blocking), the defender moves his/her hands away from the attack (see figure.27), which not only exposes a new target but also takes up valuable reaction time by moving in the wrong direction. It is commonly known that action is faster than reaction, with the major exception being when we know ahead of time what our opponent is going to do. However, a punch hits a target very quickly and so moving away from the attack only to come back again is inadvisable and is time that we do not have. When judged from the principles above it appears to:

- worsen one's own position;
- does little to affect the position of one's opponent;
- does no damage to the attacker; and
- does not avoid damage.

Yes, it could be argued (though inadvisably) that the block, once delivered, deals effectively with the punch. However, that would only be possible if you hadn't already been struck by the punch; a likelihood almost guaranteed by your chamber position. Furthermore, why both hands? In Taekwon-Do, I have never been given a plausible explanation for why we need to use both hands to block and I have asked **everyone**. Obviously, it is vastly preferable that we only use one hand to block whilst retaining the other to either block follow-up attacks or to counter, i.e. 'inflict damage'. However, the traditional block uses both hands so there must be a reason. Many of the poor reasons I have been given over the years include:

- It's a reaction hand to aid equilibrium and thus body mechanics.
- In a real fight you wouldn't do the whole chamber; just part of it.
- It's to protect the ribs before we block.
- It's 'traditional'.

Figure 28: The hand positions of the middle block

Used in this way, the block does not work and is actually dangerous. It puts the defender in greater danger. Many TKDers know this instinctively and suppress this instinct in order to comply with the 'tradition'. Such a cumbersome, time-inefficient response to a fast punch can only work under the particular conditions of set sparring detailed above. This may lead one to mistakenly believe that the block has no real utility other than that of pre-rehearsed set sparring. However, this would be an unfortunate misapprehension because, indeed, the middle block is very useful and is consistent with Miller's principles of close combat.

Note: we are examining the middle block **and** the KHGB in particular because these represent the core of our blocking system: dealing with both straight and circular attacks respectively. Furthermore, most of the other 'blocks' are variations on these techniques.

How a middle block works

The key to understanding the middle block is twofold:

1. The parry.

2. The jam.

A parry, unlike a block, is a method of gently redirecting force. It appears is most forms of fighting in one way or other and is prevalent in boxing, MMA, Wing-Chun, Kali, JKD, fencing, etc.

The middle block is actually a parry (top hand) and then a method of manipulating or jamming the attacker's arm (bottom circling hand) to momentarily disrupt the attacker's posture and thus provide a fleeting advantage for the defender, while lessening the attacker's chances of landing further blows (see Figure.28). The jamming hand also prevents the attacker's arm coming back to hit you again (see Figure.29). It does so by employing a concept called 'sticky hands', which relies on sensitivity rather than sight. Used as such, both hands have different, though equally essential, roles. The action is much the same as Mr Miagi's 'wax on wax off'. Employed in this way, both hands have separate roles, which combine to make the block. Think about it! If they didn't, then it would make no difference which way round the hands went. Neither would we have to learn a different chamber for both left and right blocking.

The exact position of the hands is essential to the block, however, and this is the hardest bit to grasp: it is not the blocking hand (bottom part of chamber) that is redirecting but rather the other hand (top part of chamber). The block is not a block at all but rather a way of manipulating the opponent's arm once the force has been redirected. The redirection is done via a parry and there-

Figure 29: The middle block working with a parry and a jam

fore comes from the non-blocking arm (top hand).

As previously stated, a block is a hard and direct way of impeding movement, i.e. a wall, whereas a parry is simply a way of redirecting a force, much like a matador's cape. However, as we know where the attacker's arm will be once we have redirected it, this allows us to be there ahead of time with our jamming arm and then manipulate the attacker's arm. The manipulation will twist the attacker's body, thereby disrupting their posture and momentarily hampering their ability to attack us again. As a result, it will:

- improve our position;
- worsen our opponent's position;
- avoid damage; and
- better facilitate our ability to do damage.

The formation of the chamber position can be seen to be halfway through the process, i.e. after the parry but before the jamming arm has circled into its final position. When viewed through the perspective of a parry and manipulate rather than a block, we can see that all parts of the action begin to take on a purpose, as follows:

1. The tuning of the body is to reduce the target area and momentarily get off line and therefore lessen the chances of being hit.

Figure 30: Various hand positions from chambers used in various styles

2. The reaction hand becomes a parry and is therefore the first thing to contact the punch. and

3. The blocking hand manipulates the opponent's arm, jamming it, thereby opening a target or facilitating a grappling application.

Though styles of Taekwon-Do and Karate differ on their exact chamber position (see Figure 30), they have much in common, as follows:

- There is a top hand and a bottom hand.
- The defender's arms cross or meet.
- One hand sweeps upwards like a windscreen wiper.
- They are all based on the Kung Fu concept of the crane's wing (see Figure.31).

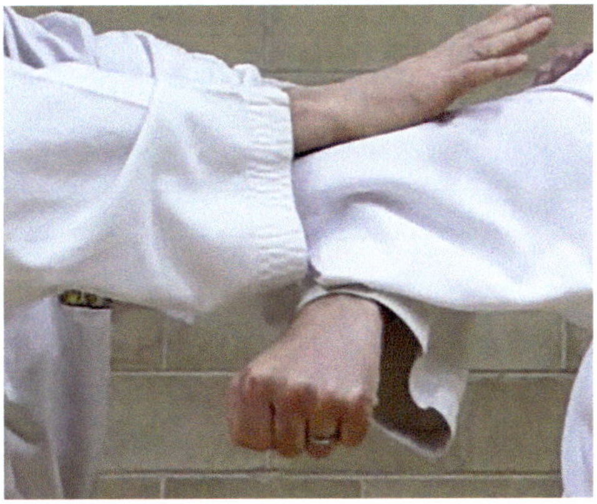

Figure 31: The cranes wing; striking pressure points on the upper forearm; and into the brachial nerve

The crane's wing

Though many styles have different interpretations of the chamber position, their commonalities are due to a common derivation: they are all based on the concept of the crane's wing. The wing not only follows the steps above but it also uses an upward sweeping action of the elbow and upper forearm of the bottom arm to redirect and possibly trap the attacker's arm. This action is still present in the Taekwon-Do middle block chamber. However, the ITF chamber requires the elbow to be lower and so its efficacy is greatly reduced. If the elbow is raised to face height, then you have a parry and trap that can effectively deal with both middle and high section straight-punch-type attacks at the same time. If the wing is dropped, then you have a structure that can deal with low section straight-line attacks such as a punch or a kick. Furthermore, at middle section the use of two arms provides both a hammer and an anvil and therefore offers the defender the ability to strike into pain receptors on the attacker's forearm should they wish to employ greater force with the parry hand (see Figure.31). This then provides a further distraction to the attacker to better facilitate effective counter techniques.

The wing options and other chambers

The beauty of the wing structure is that it uses an instinctive flinch-like response. The scissoring of the arms across the body supplies complete cover of the head and body (from the thighs up) against straight-line punches like attacks. However, how we follow up will be determined by:

- where the attacker's arm ends up; and
- what we want to do next.

In a high section attack, the attacker's arm will most likely encounter the parry hand (top hand) and be directed by it (see Figure.32). This provides the opportunity to circle up the bottom hand and jam. However, if the attack is low, then it is more likely that it is the bottom hand of the wing structure that is redirecting and therefore circling the same arm up again is not optimal owing to the fact that the opponent's arm is already travelling in the opposite direction. However, if we slide the parry arm (top hand) down the wing, we will be able to create the same disruption and jamming effect at a lower level. Here, the roles of the defender's arms are reversed, i.e. the parry arm becomes the jamming arm and vice versa. This is still a very effective response but what is of particular interest is the position of the jamming arm. It is now on top. If we ignore the stylistic tweaks of ITF Taekwon-Do, we can see that this is in fact the same chamber position as a low outer forearm block (see Figure.22). Indeed, in many styles of Japanese Karate, the chamber position employs a straight arm to better facilitate the sliding effect. Furthermore, if we employ the wing at high section but the attacker's arm is redirected by the wing instead of the parry hand, we have the option of sliding the parry arm down the wing at high section and create a high outer forearm block (see Figure 20). Again, here the chamber position, excluding ITF tweaks, is consistent with that of the Taekwon-Do block. But what if we parry the attacker's arm and we find it above our heads? The answer is simple: we use the rising block, which employs the

Figure 32: Examples of how the height of contact determines where the parry redirects

Figure 33: Being inside and outside of the opponent's arms and tools of impact

same parry and jam system, only at a new height (see Figure.30). Obviously, once we have established that the wing can be employed in blocks with a closed fist, we can also use it in blocks that have an open (knife) hand.

- Middle inner forearm block – middle reverse knife hand block
- Low outer forearm block – low knife hand block
- High outer forearm block – high knife hand (possible but chamber position is different owing to standardisation of the ITF system)

Inside vs. outside

Another quality of the wing/parry system is that it gives us options should we wish to be inside or outside our opponent's arms (see Figure.33). Obviously being inside our opponent's arms gives us more target options for countering. Conversely, it also provides the opponent with greater ability to inflict more damage on us. Whereas being on the outside of the opponent's arms gives us fewer targets, it affords us the protection of our opponent being in a disrupted posture and momentarily unable to effectively generate power. Therefore, it is much safer to be on the outside of an opponent rather that the inside where all the attacking tools are pointing at us. However, it is not always possible to choose and therefore it is wise to have a number of techniques that can deal with either position should the need arise.

The wing is such a fundamental part of blocking that it is amazing how it has been lost. The scissor action of the wing/parry structure means that it covers a very large area. This means that the defender need not necessarily be certain where the attack is aimed in order for it to be effectively dealt with. The strength of the wing shape is that it can be employed at all heights (high, middle and low section). The wing can therefore effectively deal with:

- A straight punch.
- A push.
- A grab to hair or clothing.
- A poke.
- A stab.
- A front kick.
- A side kick.
- A pushing kick.

Another strength of the wing is that it very closely resembles the body's natural flinch-like reaction and when high is extremely similar to the chamber position of the KHGB (covered later in detail).

The wing in Taekwon-Do sparring

The wing structure and the parry/jam system is difficult to conceptualise for many TKDers owing to their years of hard blocking and indoctrination into ITF dogma on what the middle block is. Ironically, it is a lack of previous exposure to middle blocking that means that teaching beginners these concepts is far easier that teaching experienced TKDers. However, grasping the concept of the wing should not be as difficult to TKDers as it is, owing to its occurrence in the sporting element of Taekwon-Do, i.e. free sparring. Indeed, the wing is often employed to close a guard in sparring

Figure 34: The scissor action of the sparring guard

(see Figure.34). Though there are many Taekwon-Do guards, the one most commonly adopted is a rear hand held high to deal with head attacks and an arm held low (bent or straight) to deal with low attacks. For defence against middle section attacks, it is a common practice to close the guard in a scissoring action, which effectively redirects or traps (illegal in ITF sparring rules) any straight-line attack at any height.

The parry system used in the wing and in sparring is a far more energy-efficient method of dealing with kicks than the hard blocking of Shotokan. It is far easier to redirect force than to spend many years conditioning the smaller weaker bones of the hand and forearm in order to risk the potentially career ending injuries that are likely to occur if one blocks full force kicks with the lower arm. This is why in Thai boxing or MMA you never see fighters attempt to block kicks in this way. If the strategy of blocking **must** be used, it is far less risky to condition and use the tibia for use against another tibia; a deduction demonstrably borne out by the preference of this strategy in sports whose rules permit full contact low kicking.

However, it is important to realise that, though present in a sport, the middle block and wing were not designed to be used in a sporting arena. They were in fact designed to be used against people who had little or no knowledge of martial arts and so the chances of such techniques working were greatly increased (Itosu's 10 Precepts). This is one reason why the martial arts were shrouded in mystery and were kept as sworn family secrets. Such techniques do not work well against skilled martial artists and experienced brawlers. This is why you do not see them in MMA or boxing. Furthermore, it does not work well against a hook punch or a circular attack. However, for many such attacks, the KHGB can be effectively employed. The wing system does, however, work effectively against thrusts from weapons and can be seen in many Kung Fu manuals as a method of trapping and disarming unskilled attackers who commit to a big thrusting attack. Originating from weapons-based systems, the parry redirect or parry trap can also be seen in many forms of Kung Fu or other East Asian systems such as Silat, Kali, Escrima and Wing-Chung.

In contrast with the ITF version of the chamber/block, positive points of the wing are that it:

- can be used at all heights (excluding below the knees);
- can be used against all straight-line attacks;
- can provide many options for counter attacking;
- uses both hands effectively;
- can be used against knives because they are derived from a weapons-based system;
- moves hands toward punch instead of away; and
- positions the body to reduce target area rather than open new targets.

The knife hand guarding block (KHGB)

The KHGB is an excellent technique and is extremely effective at dealing with circular attacks such as a hook punch. However, in Taekwon-Do its efficacy is (like the middle block) hampered by a misunderstanding of its application and failure to grasp the role that the chamber plays.

Like the middle block, the ITF explanation of KHGB is that it is used against a straight punch. This presumably is because, like the middle block, its use is derived from set sparring and therefore a need to deal with an attacker who is stepping forwards in a walking stance. Such an action lends itself well to a straight punch but not a circular attack such as a hook. Furthermore, the Chang-Hon Tuls contain many circular techniques but **no** true hook punches, i.e. the type of punch most likely to be encountered in the 'real world'. Such a misapplication is unfortunate because the KHGB is less effective against a straight punch but is instead perfectly suited to a circular attack, as will be shown.

The chamber of the KHGB

As with the above example of the middle block, the ITF KHGB chamber:

1. Wastes valuable reaction time by drawing the blocking hands away from the attacking tool.
2. Fails to explain why we need both hands.

Figure 35: The KHGB and its relation to the flinch/chamber

3. Exposes new targets to the straight punch.

However, the key to the efficacy of the KHGB is indeed the chamber. Like the middle block, the chamber **is** the block. It is based on a flinch-like reaction (see Figure.35). The hands are drawn across the body; one at face height and the other slightly lower. As before, both hands play an essential role.

Hand positions: the fence and the mother and child

In situations when we know there will be violence, it is standard self-defence practice to raise your hands in front of you to create an invisible perimeter around you. If the attacker is to do you harm, they must first breach this perimeter. In self-defence parlance, this is referred to as a fence (Thompson, 1997). The maintenance of fence guarantees one's safety and a threat to its integrity should result in a pre-emptive strike or evasion (see Figure.36). The fence usually takes the form of one hand held out in front and the other held back to add further protection or to strike should this become necessary. For the structure to be most effective, it is important that both hands are held in front of the body, elbows in. The hands work in tandem and should the back hand need to be extended then the front arm will retract to provide cover again. This concept of two interdependent hands is referred to in Chinese martial arts as 'mother and child hands' (McCarthy, 2018). A good mother would never stray too far away from her child and vice versa. The same relationship can be seen in a number of common blocks:

- Double forearm block.

Figure 36: The fence used to trigger a pre-emptive strike and its similarity to the KHGB

- KHGB.
- Forearm guarding block.
- Low KHGB.

What makes the fence structure so interesting to TKDers is that it **is** the KHGB chamber. If you take up a fence and then just turn your head to your back shoulder, you will see that your hands are neatly positioned as they would be were you in the process of guarding down towards that shoulder (see Figure.35). Furthermore, the use of this structure as a 'fence' is common to many martial arts.

Though variations of this chamber can be seen when comparing many arts, the differences turns out to be mainly stylistic. In arts that contain this technique, the main principles of the mother and child concept remain consistent. The hands move interdependently with one hand covering for the other. The fence structure also works well with the parry and jam system or the full wing and trap.

Figure 37: The KHGB chamber used to stop a punch and the block used to strike the neck

KHGB: the chamber is the block

Unlike many other blocks, the KHGB chamber is also exactly the same shape as the final block. This should make it obvious that the chamber is in fact just another KHGB. When inspecting the final hand positions of the KHGB, it becomes obvious that the position of the back hand is curious. Why is the palm turned upright and why is it held at the solar plexus rather than further away from the body? The answer to this conundrum is twofold:

1. Standardisation.
2. Application.

Standardisation: the KHGB actually has many chamber positions in other Karate and Kung Fu-based arts. The different chambers represent both the personal preference of the style's originator and the different applications of the block. It is unfortunate that, in the need to standardise arts and make them more teachable, a lot of the richness in variety is lost. This is why TKDers have adopted only one chamber for the KHGB and eschewed the other possibilities. Such standardisation has the drawback of limiting applications for the technique and therefore makes interpreting the kata templates, most of which predate the standardisation, very difficult and confusing.

Application: a common explanation for why the ITF KHGB has the hands in the position it does is that, once the hook punch has been blocked, the attacker's arm is wrapped and the knife hand is driven into the side of the attacker's neck (see Figure.37). The wrapping of the arm leaves the blocker with a palm facing up and at solar plexus level whilst the KHGB is angled to squeeze between the shoulder and the jaw. Such a position not only provides the defender with a good counter but gives them excellent control over the attacker to further strike or follow up with grappling-based techniques. Though the small section of the hand between the wrist and the base of the small finger is commonly utilised as the striking/blocking tool in TKD, the long bone of the ulna is much more effective and durable when slammed into the neck. Therefore, the same technique is just as effective with a closed fist in a forearm guarding block.

The same technique can be seen in other martial arts and the final position of the arm and hand may vary. In some styles/arts it may look more like a palm strike than a KHGB. However, it is more the intention than the hand position that dictates efficacy.

KHGB: other chambers and uses

One of the alternative chamber positions still used in many forms of Karate is that of the high straight arm and crossed arm position similar to an extended middle block chamber. Again, one

Figure 38: Example of using a variation on the chamber to enable a strike to brachial nerve

can see both the derivation from the wing and the resemblance of the natural flinch position. The advantage of this chamber when used against a hook punch is that, once the punch has been stopped, the other, so far unused, arm is able to slide down the defender's arm and strike into the attacker's bicep. Though this will not completely disable the attacker, if delivered in the correct location with the correct level of intensity, it can effect an electric-shock-like symptom by over-stimulating/striking the brachial nerve in the bicep muscle (see Figure.38). Though not a fight stopper, the effect of such a strike may be to temporarily deaden the arm or at least to distract the attacker long enough to effect a successful counter or escape. Unfortunately, this use has been lost in Taekwon-Do owing to its reliance on a single KHGB chamber position that does not facilitate the action.

The KHGB, the flinch and S.P.E.A.R.

As mentioned earlier, the body has natural inbuilt reactions to sudden threats, which operate faster than conscious thought. We term these 'flinches' and the KHGB chamber is one such reaction (see Figure 24). Indeed, so effective is this structure at staving off single attacks that modern martial arts guru and successful entrepreneur Tony Blauer has built an entire system of self-defence around it. According to Wikipedia:

> *"The SPEAR System (an acronym for Spontaneous Protection Enabling Accelerated Response) is a close-quarter protection system that uses a person's reflex action in threatening situations as a basis for defence. The founder, Tony Blauer, developed the SPEAR System in Canada during the 1980s. It has since been adopted by several military and law enforcement agencies across the world."* (Wikipedia, 2018)

Figure 39: Tony Blauer's S.P.E.A.R. system and its use of the KHGB as a control position

However, what makes this extremely popular and effective system so relevant to Taekwon-Do is that it is built completely around the KHGB and its chamber; further proof if needed that the old methods are just as effective today as they have always been.

So, to summarise:

The two main blocks of the ITF system can be seen to be:

1. The middle block in its check and bridge form (or contained within the full wing structure) and its derivatives – used against a straight attack.
2. The KHGB with the chamber forming the actual block and the follow-up being used as a strike and arm control – used predominantly against circular attacks.

The commonalities are:

- Both blocks operate at realistic engagement distances
- Both bocks utilise the body's natural flinch-like reactions
- Both blocks improve the defender's position
- Both blocks worsen the attacker's position
- Both blocks effective utilise both hands in an interdependent way

Though it is important to reiterate that there definitely is blocking within the pre-war Okinawan Karate and therefore within the Chang-Hon Tuls which are derived from it, the vast majority of so-called blocks are either used incorrectly or were never blocks at all.

Ambiguities and blocking

One issue that compounds the problems of interpreting the collective applications of the multitude of blocks is that quite often there is no single correct application. This is a conceptual issue for the Western mindset, which does not deal well with ambiguity but instead prefers definitive answers. Unfortunately, ambiguity is the preferred state of blocking because the applications of the blocks are only limited by three factors:

1. The constraints of body.
2. The context.
3. The imagination.

Body and imagination: the body makes limited movements. Our elbows only hinge one way, our shoulders rotate but don't detach, our wrists rotate but have a greater range of movement up and down than left and right. These rules are common to the majority of humans. However, the tasks we can employ these limited movements for are infinite. Operating within the same mechanical restrictions, we may use the motions to paint the Sistine chapel or simply brush our teeth. As a result, when displaying patterns of movement such as an outstretched arm, a kata/tul may be representing numerous common defensive or offensive actions. Furthermore, the standardisation of techniques means that the body shapes contained within tuls are limited to representing the ideal shapes contained within the *Encyclopaedia*. However, what these shapes can and are applied to is far less limited and is decided more by context.

Context: When one uses one's body to defend oneself, it is the context that dictates the response; **not** dogma. The applications of the patterns are based on principles and may be modified to suit the context whilst remaining consistent with the original intent, for example:

Relevance: a high kick is not an adequate response to a bear hug or a head lock. Applications tend to be designed to help deal with a specific threat rather than a general one.

Appropriacy: someone dragging you into a car or someone simply pulling you on to the dance floor may require different responses. Could one justifiably blind both people? Could the same technique be modified to deal with both threats?

Body shape: some techniques are better suited to certain body types. Will a small woman or a child be able to shoulder throw a 20-stone rugby player? Will a 20-stone rugby player have the same flexibility and therefore be able to kick as high as the lady or the child?

Funakoshi said that the techniques may change but the principles never vary. To illustrate this point and to further elucidate the mystery of the Chang-Hong Tuls, we will now look at a small number of blocks and how, by using the same principles, they can be effectively used to apply a variety of responses to common attacks.

The blocks: their principles and their applications

Block 1: Low pressing block – Principles and analysis

Perhaps the block with the least plausible and most incomplete explanation in Taekwon-Do orthodoxy is the 'low pressing block' (see Figure.40). This block is executed by:

1. Raising the hands.
2. Shifting the weight of the body on to one foot.
3. Moving the hands in opposite directions and in slow motion whilst lowering the body into a low stance (slightly longer than a walking stance).

Figure 40: Low pressing block

Current ITF thought is that one hand is blocking a kick whilst the other is simultaneously blocking a punch. If we leave aside the highly improbable scenario of an attacker both kicking and punching at the same time (very difficult to pull off and to do so prevents body mechanics from generating power), this explanation fails on many fronts, as follows:

- It fails to 'press' anything. The name of the block (pressing block) would imply a pressing action.
- It fails to explain why we are in slow motion.
- It fails to explain why we are in a low stance and not just a walking stance.
- It fails to explain why we are exerting power in a downwards motion and why our low hand is in a knife hand position (the position now favoured by certain ITF groups over the old flat palm position with a bent wrist).
- It fails to effectively deal with either a punch or a kick because the low kick would break our fingers and the punch would still travel forward unimpeded.

Far more satisfactory explanations are that:

- We are actually 'pressing' something.
- We are creating a lever to exert pressure over something in a downward motion by pressing it.
- The hand that rises is securing something and, by rising, it increases the leverage over the object.
- It is executed in a low stance because dropping our weight through the technique increases the downward pressure.
- The block is done in slow motion because it is a form of joint lock and **not** a break. The same technique could be performed much faster if the intention was to destroy the limb or joint. This is a controlling technique; not an impact technique

In the first application we will see that all of the above principles are addressed.

Low pressing block: Application A (used against a round kick (turning kick) – pressing the knee takedown)

This technique is used against a round kick (see Figure.41). Instead of offering the small bones of the forearm to block this powerful kick, we are going to use rudimentary physics and catch the kick at the optimal velocity, i.e. when it is slowing down and has passed its intended point of impact. To achieve this we will simply step round on the arc of the kick away from the focus of power. This will enable us to catch the kick without sustaining too much damage. Once the leg has been captured, the takedown is achieved by use of the lever action of the pressing block. One hand will pressure down through the knee while the other will hold the leg of the attacker with an upturned palm. This takedown can be performed by simply stepping into a long, low stance or (as in this variation) by first stepping behind the attacker's standing leg to prevent their readjustment.

The Steps

1. The attacker throws a round kick to the ribs. The defender steps round on the arc of the kick to avoid its power.

2. As the kick makes contact with the defenders ribs he/she wraps his/her arm over the leg securing a good hold.

3. The defender then places his/her free palm on the knee of the attacker's trapped leg and further strengthens the control.

Option 1: The defender can now simply step forward into a low stance whilst applying downward pressure to the knee to affect a takedown.

Option 2: To prevent the attacker hopping around and maintaining balance the defender can step behind the attacker's standing leg and block it. This will cause the defender to adopt more of a sitting stance when affecting the takedown. Again the defender will pressure through the knee to disrupt the attacker's balance.

Follow-up: Once the attacker is on the floor the defender can simply throw the leg to one side to disengage. However, if the goal is further control the defender can:

1. Step on the attackers free leg to avoid being kicked by it.

2. Turn the arm holding the leg so that the bone of the forearm is pressing against the attacker's Achilles tendon.

3. By arching his/her back the defender can attack the tendon of the attacker's leg. This can be used for pain compliance or to destroy the leg depending on the circumstances and justified level of force.

As can be seen from this application, all the constituent parts of the block are fully explained and utilised. This makes it a far more satisfactory application than the simultaneous blocking of a kick and a punch.

Figure 41: Pressing the knee takedown using the lever action of the pressing block

Low pressing block: Application B (used against a hook punch – pressing the head takedown)

As has been previously stated, the context is the biggest deciding factor in how a technique is applied. If the context changes then so does the application, for example, have you been attacked with a grab, a kick or a punch? The same technique can also be used to take down an opponent from a caught kick by pressing the knee (see Figure.42). However, we will now look at pressing the head as a response to a hook punch. But it is important to realise that in both examples the principles of leverage are consistent with the previous move: one arm elevates whilst the other applies constant pressure.

Figure 42: Pressing the head takedown from a hook punch

The steps

1. The attacker throws a hook punch.
2. The defender blocks the punch with a KHGB.
3. The defender wraps the arm and immediately slams the other forearm into the neck of the attacker.
4. The defender knees the attacker in the groin and then circles one hand up and under the attacker's punching arm whilst placing the other palm on the back of the attacker's neck/ head.

Block 2: Nine-shaped block – principles and analysis

This block, not encountered until black belt, is proposed as a method of breaking a wrist (see Figure.43). The defender is supposedly attacked with a straight punch or a grab to the centre of a garment. In response, the defender raises one arm and lowers the other. Both arms are then scissored in a fast action whilst the defender lowers him/herself into a sitting stance. The idea is that the scissoring wrists of the defender break the wrist of the attacker. This false explanation has been allowed to persist due to the inability of students to test the veracity of the claim that it would actually break the attacker's wrist and **not** the defender's. It fails on a number of fronts:

Figure 43: The 9-shaped block and its implausible application to break a wrist

- Standing in front of a violent attacker in a sitting stance where you are immobile and very vulnerable in terms of open targets is unwise. A sitting stance should be used to drop weight through an attacker whilst holding them, thereby rendering them incapable of movement and unpredictable attacks.
- The wrists of the defender would need to pass each other so closely to exert the pressure on the correct locations of the attacker's wrist as to make it more likely that the defender would smash his/her own hands together. Indeed, anyone who has trained Po-Eun, Gae-baek or Yoo-Sin will attest to how frequently this happens without a violent attacker to complicate things.

However, a technique commonly used in Ju-Jitsu and Chin-Na that employs the same sitting stance and scissoring motion is described below (see Figure.44). Here, the scissoring action is used to break or dislocate an elbow. This technique is usually done in slow motion for training purposes or to exert control through pain compliance. However, if executed quickly, as in Taekwon-Do, it will destroy the joint of the attacker. The hand that rises to the top position is used to apply pressure to the triceps tendon and to secure a garment for leverage whilst the other arm operates the lever by pulling the attacker's arm in a downward motion. The sitting stance is used to create a stable base behind the attacker and to prevent them from stepping backwards to alleviate the pressure/pain. In this application, all parts of the technique are utilised and explained.

Figure 44: 9-shaped block used to attack the elbow joint

Nine-shaped block: Application A (used against a cross wrist grab)

The steps

1. The defender's wrist is seized. The defender reverses the position and secures hold of the attacker's wrist (not shown above).
2. The defender turns sideways and punches across the face of the attacker to stretch them out (as in Po-Eun).
3. If the attacker is taller, then the defender will need to break his posture. This can be done by forming a KHGB shape and driving the elbow into the depression where the clavicle meets the deltoid.
4. The defender drops his weight down through the attacker, circles his free arm over the attacker's arm and continues up and behind the attacker's triceps.
5. The defender secures a tight grip on his own garment to completely immobilise and isolate the attacker's arm and at the same time drives the attacker's wrist down and round in a circle to destroy the elbow joint.

Again, in this application one can see the need to be in a sitting stance to provide stability and to drag the opponent down. The scissoring action of both hands makes sense in conjunction with the levering motion of the elbow destruction. In short, all parts of the technique support the application rather than appear mysterious or dangerous to the defender, as in the ITF application.

Block 3: U-shaped block – principles and analysis

The next technique to face analytical scrutiny is the U-shaped block (Digutcha Makgi) (see Figure.45). The ITF application for this is perhaps the most implausible of all those offered. We are expected to believe that the block is used to disarm an attacker brandishing a bo staff. In patterns, such as Joong-Gun where the technique appears in pairs, we are expected to believe that, after acquiring the weapon, we then throw it away using the same block. Let us examine why this is so implausible:

Figure 45: The U-shaped block

- Why in a weaponless (empty handed) system are we suddenly defending against a bo staff? Why not a knife or a gun? Two weapons that were and are far more prevalent in post-World War II Korea than a bo staff.
- Why do we throw away a weapon we have managed to acquire? Better to turn it on our attacker.
- Why is our attacker so close to us? The bo staff is a distance weapon.
- Why are we doing this in a fixed stance?
- Why are we turning our back on our attacker whilst throwing the staff? Shouldn't we be hitting them and incapacitating them first? Might they not attack us while our back was turned?
- Why are we throwing a weapon using such a cumbersome and ineffective method? It would be better to throw it like a javelin, which would propel it further.

The answer to all these questions is simple: the action has nothing to do with a bo staff. The bo staff application is another that has been inherited from Shotokan Karate. It is undocumented but highly probable that this may be down to a misinterpretation and that at some point someone may have said: "It's **as if** you are taking a bo staff and throwing it." However, we will never know. What is documented is that the technique can be used as:

1. A takedown from a front kick, as commonly taught in classical Ju-Jitsu (Figure.46).

2. A simultaneous strike to groin and throat, as depicted in the drawings of the ancient Karate masters' text, the Bubishi (not covered here).

3. An effective escape from a headlock (side chancery) (Figure.47).

U-shaped block: Application A (takedown - against a front kick)

The steps

1. The attacker attempts a footballer-style front kick following through with the leg, as unskilled people tend to.

2. The defender turns his/her body so that they are off line and then catches the outstretched leg of the attacker.

3. The defender places his hand on the attacker's face (though a strike to the neck is equally effective).

4. The defender drives both arms towards the attacker transferring his/her weight in the new direction. This has the effect of lifting the attacker's leg higher than balance permits whilst thrusting them backwards and ultimately to the floor.

Figure 46: U-shaped block used as a takedown from a front kick

U-shaped block: Application B (takedown - used against a head lock [side chancery])

Here, the attacker is in a chancery headlock: an instinctive grappling move, and very much the type that schoolchildren effect whilst wrestling. However, that is not to say that this technique is to be take for granted. In 'real' self-defence, the danger is that the attacker may be punching you in the face whilst holding your head in this dangerous position. Another risk is that the circulation/breathing is cut off and unconsciousness or death become a possibility. Obviously, the greater the time spent in the headlock, the greater the risk that you will be hurt by the attacker or his/her friends. It is for this reason that escaping quickly is essential, and the U-shaped block provides a simple way to achieve this end.

The steps

1. The defender first grabs the attacker's arm and pulls down to open a space and prevent choking.

2. The defender turns his head to keep the forearm off his windpipe and then bites into the attacker's side to distract him.

3. The defender inserts one arm between the defender's legs and brings the other up behind the attacker's back to attack the face. The nose can be grabbed for good leverage or for more extreme measures the eye or the mouth can be fishhooked.

4. Attacking the face causes the defender to recoil and breaks his/her posture. By continuing with the pressure to the face and simultaneously lifting the attacker's leg, an effective takedown can be achieved.

5. If the attacker stubbornly refuses to fall, then his/her supporting leg can be swept too, as in Sam Il Tul.

Figure 47: Escape from a headlock using two U-shaped blocks

Block 4: Wedging block (and front snap kick double punch)

The last block we shall look at is the wedging block (see Figure.48). This is often mistakenly used to escape from a double collar grab. Though this may work if preceded by a kick to the testes, it is not the best way to remove such a grab and, indeed, without such a 'softener' it simply does not generate enough leverage to effect an escape from a determined attacker. However, the wedging block does work very well against two common acts of violence, as follows:

1. A two-handed shove.

2. A same side wrist grab.

Figure 48: Wedging block front snap kick double punch

Note: This version sacrifices stylistic aesthetics in order to generate maximum power in punches

Wedging block: Application A (the two-handed shove)

This is a very common act of violence. As Miller points out, it is part of the 'monkey dance' and is often an expression of social violence (Miller, 2011). Therefore, it may be an act of threat with the intention of avoiding real violence. However, it is unpleasant and can be easily dealt with using a technique referred to in Chin-Na as a 'dissolve' (see Figure.49). Furthermore, the mechanics of the attack are similar to attempts to grab the throat or the lapels, so the same defence can be used for all three attacks.

The steps

1. As the attacker draws back and squares up to ready for a shove, the defender is able to recognise the tell-tale signs.

2. As the attacker extends his arms into the shove, the defender brings his up through the middle

and circles them out to dissipate the force of the attack whilst remaining in contact with the attacker's arms (i.e. a dissolve).

3. The defender immediately secures control of the attacker's sleeves or wrists and, whilst holding them apart, delivers a kick to the groin.
4. As the attacker bends forward, the defender is then able to attack the head with a control technique or a series of punches, as in Do-San Tul.

Figure 49: A dissolve from a two-handed shove using the wedging block

Wedging block: Application B (centre lock against a same side wrist grab)

A wrist grab is a technique that any competent martial artist should know how to deal with. There are many ways of doing so. This technique employs a 'centre lock' to control the attacker. The angle of the centre lock requires the defender to turn into the attacker at roughly 45 degrees. The turning motion gives a far better explanation for the sequence in Do-San Tul, which requires the defender to turn and step at 45 degrees (see Figure.50).

The steps

1. The attacker has grabbed the defender's wrist in a same side grab. The defender, using his free hand, immediately clamps the attacker's hand.
2. The defender turns to the side of the attacker and swings his elbow over the attacker's to keep it down and to maintain the pressure whilst rotating the attacker's wrist.
3. The defender removes the hand that was originally grabbed and slides it down the attacker's arm. The defender then hooks with two fingers in the crook of the attacker's elbow in an action often referred to as 'bird plucks a branch'.
4. The defender turns in at 45 degrees to bend the arm. Simultaneously, the defender will pull the crook of the arm whilst rotating the attacker's hand in the opposite direction. This causes the wrist to lock out and results in great pain.
5. The attacker will usually drop to their knees to alleviate the pain, thereby providing the face as a target for the defender to front kick.
6. As the head comes up from the kick, it provides a further target for a series of punches.

Figure 50: (Opposite page) A centre lock from a same side wrist grab using a wedging block

So to summarise:

As can be seen from the above examples, when we examine the specific qualities of each so-called' block', we can see that these same properties can be used to great effect for a number of non-blocking applications. Without getting into the controversial area of whether General Choi was right or wrong in his understanding of the nature of Karate blocking, we can safely conclude that:

- Taekwon-Do was derived from Shotokan, which was derived from old school Karate.
- The blocks are older than Taekwon-Do and modern Karate and appear in many ancient kata.
- The applications offered above are common to many complete arts which encompass rudimentary grappling, including old school Karate.
- It is highly probable that many of the so-called 'blocks' are in fact grappling and controlling techniques. Old school Karate supports this view.
- Explanations of the Taekwon-Do patterns are at best incomplete so it is not disloyal to question them and test their rigour.
- We should look beyond the given explanations if we wish to truly understand our art.
- A good source of applications for the TKD patterns is old school Karate

When viewed in these terms, the patterns come alive and a whole new avenue of study becomes available to us; the Japanese for which is known as 'bunkai'. Furthermore, once we begin to revaluate the methods of blocking that we were given, we can begin to sift the wheat from the chaff. This will not only leave us with a very effective method of dealing with percussive impact, i.e. blocking, but also a whole host of methods of dealing with the myriad forms of violent physical attacks that one may encounter. By addressing these issues, the beautiful art of Taekwon-Do may at last live up to its claim that it is also the most effective method of self-defence.

태권도

Chapter 3: Stances:

It's not how you stand that is important but rather what you stand for

Figure 51: Stance training as stress positions (Drunken Master, 1978)

Another area of traditional 'training' that has taken a radical departure from 'effective' training is that of stance training. In Taekwon-Do and so-called 'traditional Karate', stance training is the embodiment of function over form. Many hours are dedicated to the practice of achieving the unobtainable perfect stance and much, much less time is directed to the arguably more important aim of understanding what they are for. Throughout the history of modern arts like Taekwon-Do the student has been distracted from the real purpose of stances with obfuscating advice that stances are for strength training of legs and not for actual combat (see Figure.51). Furthermore, the emphasis on stances is always as static forms rather than as dynamic methods of energy transference. When one begins to define the true and multiple purposes of stances and examines these purposes through the prism of actual combat, one can see why so many exist and what it is about their particular use that causes the differentiation in the main properties of stances, i.e. stability, mobility and transference of energy. Stances should be viewed not as ends in themselves but as vectors for:

- delivering force;
- avoiding force;
- holding/anchoring;
- moving oneself;
- moving others; and

- all the other challenges one may encounter in prearranged physical combat or non-consensual physical violence.

Many modern arts, such as MMA, Muay Thai and Western boxing, focus very little on what TKDers would recognise as proper stance training yet their arts can be seen to be devastatingly effective in actual combat against non-compliant opponents. This leads many such athletes to be very critical of the type of stance training found in modern Karate and Taekwon-Do. However, it is wrong to conflate the value of 'stance training' with the value of actual 'stances' and to do so is to throw the baby out with the bath water. Indeed, many 'warriors' of the 'Octagon' are ignorant of the fact that in any given bout they will transition though the vast majority of classical stances from L-stance to bending stance going through sitting stance and even X-stance along the way (see Figure.52). What's more, it is only by looking at such dynamic grappling-based arts that we can begin to understand why we place such emphasis on these wonderful ways of moving.

Figure 52: Various stances at use in MMA

Fighting: dynamic vs static

Karate legend Nakamura was often quoted as saying: "You don't fight in a stance; you finish fights in a stance" (Miller, 2011). This single statement sums up the dichotomy of stances and their traditional method of training; namely one is dynamic and the other is static. Fighting is by its very nature a frenetic and dynamic pursuit. Controlling one's own movement in a fight is very difficult to do; especially because of the added complication of a violent partner(s) exerting force upon you in a determined yet unpredictable manner. There is overwhelming CCTV evidence to show that most fights, if not finished in the first few blows, inevitably devolve into some kind of grappling scenario (see Figure.53). Creating distance and slugging it out in an orderly exchange of blows is learnt behaviour; not inherent.

Figure 53: Examples of the brutality of real world violence and its frenetic nature

However, grabbing and pulling and seeking to control through strength is a natural behaviour and is pre-programmed into us from birth (at least). All children, like bears, monkeys and most other mammals, wrestle for dominance from birth. Usually this takes the form of play. In most species, and especially in predators, this practised behaviour becomes either a way of subduing prey or a method of settling intra-tribal disputes. Philosopher Thomas Hobbs explained that, as members of society, we have signed an implied social contract, which necessitates giving up socially undesirable rights of the individual. As members of society, we agree not to fight in public to settle disputes. However, such behaviour is hardwired into us and more so in young adult males who seek to elevate their social positions through such acts of social violence. Come Friday night, the streets of most UK city centres will be full of alcohol-fuelled young men punching and wrestling. By observing such untrained behaviour, one can see the physical demands it places on the individual; how opponents vie for dominant positions through pushing, grabbing, pulling, shifting of weight, repositioning of feet to create balance and transitioning back to rudimentary striking when one's position permits. Such fights are frantic and highly dynamic and it is rare for individuals to stand still for any great length of time.

In sport, the closest we get to such 'real violence' is MMA. Here again, the same can be said that individuals seek to strike to dominate or wrestle to improve one's position and create better opportunities to strike or submit. Despite the obvious discrepancies of skill, rules and legitimacy, street fighting and MMA look quite similar in their dynamics. However, what is most relevant to the traditional martial artist is the fact that both groups use stances to affect their opponent(s). And both groups will transition through these stances at will. When one thinks of the specific demands on the body, one will realise quite quickly that you do not position your feet the same way when seeking to optimally:

- pull vs push;
- move forwards vs move sideways; and
- lift up vs drag down or backwards.

It is these major differences that give us the need for different stances. And the dynamic demands of real violence that dictate the efficacy of stances. Under such conditions, it is impossible to check if the angle of the stance is correct or if the feet are perfectly parallel. Furthermore, it is irrelevant because the goal is effective fighting; **not** conforming to an aesthetic idea.

Stance training

TMA have become obsessed with the 'Tao' or 'Do' side to the martial arts, i.e. the attempt at achieving the elusive quality of perfection and, by pursuing it, acquiring introspective knowledge and character improvement.

To achieve perfection, TMA have an exact ideal of a stance. In such arts, one's skill level is assessed by how close one can make their body conform to that ideal shape. Therefore, a huge amount of time is dedicated to standing still in this ideal shape whilst one's form is assessed by an instructor. In short, stances become 'freeze frames' by which students are judged. The pursuit of perfection in 'Do' as an objective is not without value and could arguably be rated as a more important quality of martial arts training owing to the fact that most of us inhabit a world where we can avoid violence. However, the pursuit of perfection is an objective that conflicts with the pursuit of efficacy, and herein lies the problem. Most traditional martial artists do not understand this. It is okay to practise standing around in static stances so long as you do not mistake this for effective training on how to actually use them in dynamic – and frantic – violent situations. Violence is dynamic; stance training is static. Training for one does not ready you for the other.

The conflicting objectives of stances

Above all, stances are merely methods of achieving three main objectives at their optimal level, as follows:

1. Mobility.
2. Stability.
3. Transference of energy.

Mobility: can be defined as the ability to move; whether this be to avoid damage, to improve your mechanical/positional advantage or to better deliver force.

Movement is essential in combat. It is harder to hit a moving target than a stationary one and so skills like dodging, ducking and weaving, and getting offline are tried and tested strategies of avoiding percussive impact. Such movements rely on the body's ability to shift on request. They combine circular movements of the waist with springing/sinking movements of the legs as well as the ability to step in all directions.

Stability: can be defined as the ability to resist movement or to control the destabilising effects of movement.

Stability is essential for both striking and grappling. Uncontrolled falling to the ground is a recipe for disaster in a fight and therefore one's ability to plant the feet to create a stable base is essential. The wider the base, the greater the stability one has. However, when using one's feet to create a base, one must recognise that they are quite small and do not provide great stability in all directions at the same time. Hence, when one assumes a wide stance, such as a sitting stance, one is stable in only one direction and can easily be off balanced by being pushed backwards or being pulled forwards. The same can be said for most stances that offer stability in a forwards or backwards direction, for example, an L-stance or a fixed stance. They offer little stability sideways. Whilst some stances offer stability both sideways and forwards/backwards, they are very prone to imbalance on a diagonal plane (walking stance, low stance). Therefore, selecting the correct stance is often dependent on which direction one seeks to achieve stability.

Hara and stability

Controlling one's centre of gravity ('hara' in Japanese) is also an essential element of stability. The higher the centre of gravity is, the less stable one is. So, dropping one's weight can be seen as effectively lowering mass and therefore hara. Furthermore, keeping one's hara within one's base means maintaining stability. The moment the hara travels outside of the base then stability

Figure 54: Attacking the base and shifting the mass too (o soto gari or inner reaping throw i.e. saju jirugi)

is compromised and balance undone (i.e. a takedown or a throw). It is therefore advantageous to keep our hara within our base and seek to move our opponent's outside of theirs. Attacking an opponent's balance can therefore be done effectively in one of two ways, as follows:

1. Shift the opponent's mass away from their base (pull, push, lift, drag or compel through strikes or pain).

2. Attack the opponent's base (sweep a leg, anchor base, entangle legs or prevent readjusting of base).

Doing both at the same time will therefore maximise one's chances of successfully taking an opponent to the ground (see Figure.54). It is possible to use stances not only to maintain one's own stability but as devices to attack that of an opponent.

Transference of energy: can be defined as the ability to channel kinetic energy into a specific task to affect another body. Examples include pulling, pushing, lifting, dragging down and all forms of percussive impact.

The transference of energy can be seen as the application or combination of both stability and mobility in line with the selection of the correct tool, angle, method and level of intensity (Knapp, 2009). Movement can be said to be an expression of kinetic energy, i.e. the energy of movement. All things have mass and when that mass moves there is kinetic energy. Kinetic energy is directly proportional to the mass of the object and to the square of its velocity:

$$\mathbf{KE = 1/2\ m\ v^2}$$

The kinetic energy is measured in joules and can be increased by increasing the mass. However, increasing the velocity has a far greater effect on the level of kinetic energy. By looking at the above equation we can see that:

- **doubling the mass = doubling the kinetic energy; and**
- **doubling the velocity = quadrupling the kinetic energy**

A deeper understanding of the physics of thermodynamics is beyond most of us and, to be honest, is of little real value to the martial artist. What is highly pertinent and easily 'digestible' in laymen's terms is that you can hit harder by:

- throwing more weight into your technique; and
- increasing the speed of the technique

Isaac Newton discovered that if you press on an object then that object presses back upon you. He proposed that both things press with an equal force. He summed this up with the equation:

FA=-FB

Here, Force A is equal to Force B, but in the opposite direction. This is commonly summed up as "for every action there is an equal and opposite reaction". This is Newton's Third Law of motion. Again, this is too complex for many of us to fully comprehend and arguably unnecessary too. However, we can simplify the physics for our purposes and simply accept that:

1. The ground gives us energy.
2. As we press down on the earth it presses back on us. and
3. Because the ground is heavier than us, we are able to use its force to generate our movement.

(Tigon, 2019)

So, in martial arts we can state that: "Movement begins from the ground". Thus our relationship with the ground impacts our movement and our ability to transfer energy.

Stability and mobility: movement in martial arts

Body movement is a serious of segmental interactions of stability and mobility. The various structures of the body (muscles, bones, ligaments tendons, etc.) must be stabilised, and their stiffness must be released sequentially at just the right time to permit movement (McDonald, 2016). These movements are all deriving energy from the ground. In biomechanics terms, this is called the 'ground reaction force' (GRF). For us to effectively channel this, our feet must be grounded, i.e. they must be effectively connected to the earth. A boxer may be light on his/her toes when moving but, when delivering knockout blows, his/her feet have a greater connection with the canvas of the ring and they use their huge leg muscles to push off and punch with real power.

So, to summarise:

- We derive our energy from the ground.
- How we position our feet on the ground will affect the efficiency of that energy transfer.
- To deliver this energy we require a combination of both stability and mobility.

The conflict of stability and mobility

When we look at most stable structures, we can see that there is little movement in them. Think of a house or the trunk of a tree; both express their strength as an ability to resist movement. Conversely, the more mobile a structure is the less connection it appears to have with the earth. Think of leaves on the tree or a discarded carrier bag blowing in the wind. The same is true when we think about our stances. A stance that is very stable has a greater connection with the earth and so inherently lacks mobility, for example, a sitting stance. Whereas a stance that is highly mobile has less connection with the earth and is far less stable. Think of a sparring stance in which one is bouncing. It is not possible to be completely mobile and completely stable at the same time. Neither is it possible to be stable in all directions at the same time (without assistance). Therefore, the efficiency of a stance can be seen to be a trade-off between these two qualities. So, one must compromise when selecting a stance. One guiding principle that helps in such a selection is: 'Is it the right tool for the job?'

Auxiliary uses of stances

As well as stability, mobility and energy transfer, the stance itself can have certain extra qualities that permit us to use it against an opponent. Some of these auxiliary uses include:

- trapping the leg of an opponent;
- sweeping the legs of an opponent;
- popping the knee out of an opponent to attack balance;
- trapping the feet of an opponent to restrict movement or to damage the leg/foot;
- reducing the target area, i.e. angling of body or placing a leg in front of groin; and
- increasing reach by bringing the front foot closer and/or extending the stance.

The Stances

According to the condensed *Encyclopaedia* 1988–99, there are 13 major stances in Taekwon-Do (see Table 3) plus some variations. Nearly all have of these have direct equivalents in Japanese and differ very little from the Shotokan versions from which they were derived. Exceptions to this are the walking stance and the front stance (see Figure ??). The walking stance has a 50:50 weight distribution whereas the Shotokan version is usually 60:40 (explained later).

Table 3: The Major Stances of Taekwon-Do and Shotokan Karate

	Taekwon-Do Stance	Korean Term	Shotokan Version	Japanese Translation
1.	Sitting stance	Annun Sogi	Kiba Dachi	Horse stance
2.	Walking stance	Gunnun Sogi	Zenkutsu Dachi	Front stance
3.	Low stance	Nachuo Sogi	None	Not found
4.	L-stance	Niunja Soji	Kokutsu Dachi	Back stance
5.	Fixed stance	Gojung Sogi	Like Fudo Dachi	Immovable stance
6.	X-stance	Kyocha Sogi	Kosa Dachi	Cross-legged stance
7.	Bending stance	Guburyo Sogi	Tsuru Ashi Dachi	Crane leg stance
8.	One-leg stance	Waebal Sogi	Tsuru Ashi Dachi	Crane leg stance (variation)
9.	Rear-foot stance	Dwitbal Sogi	Neko Ashi Dachi	Cat stance
10	Parallel Stance	Narani Sogi	Heiko Dachi	Parallel stance
11.	Vertical stance	Soojik Sogi	Renoji Dachi	L-stance
12.	Attention stance*	Charyot Sogi	Musubi Dachi	Informal attention stance
13.	Closed stance*	Moa Sogi	Heisoku Dachi	Closed leg stance
14.	Not in TKD	–	Shiko Dachi	Sumo stance
15.	Not in TKD	–	Sanchin Dachi	From the Kata Sanchin
*Not covered because proper ties are so similar to parallel stance				

Listed below are other stances that feature in the *Encyclopaedia*. However, they do not appear frequently in the patterns.

- **Diagonal stance (Sesun Sogi)**: this can be seen to be a variation of the sitting stance with the feet slightly offset

- **Crouched stance (Oguryo Sogi)** (Hangetsu Dachi in Japanese): this is the wider Shotokan variation of the much narrower Sanchin Dachi, which is commonly used in the Kata Sanchin (a signature kata of Goju Ryu)
- **Open stance** (Palji stance): outer and inner

Variations of major stances

Many of the major stances also have variations, such as:

- Ready
- Jumbi
- Warrior
- A to D labels

However, these are merely changes of hand positions and not feet or weight distribution and so do not really constitute different stances. One interesting omission is the lack of a Taekwon-Do equivalent for Shiko Dachi. This is a version of the sitting stance with the feet pointing out at roughly 45 degrees. Adjusting the feet like this is very useful in order to resist being pulled off balance whilst in a sitting stance. However, as it is the main contention of this book that stances have distinct combative properties, let us now turn our eye to the individual stances and their purposes.

Analysis and combative examples of the stances

1. Sitting Stance

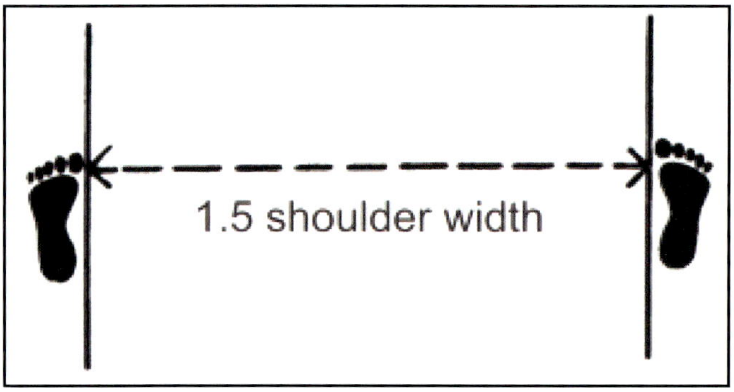

- One and a half shoulder widths between big toes
- Weight distribution 50:50
- Both feet pointing forwards
- Kneecaps over balls of feet
- Grip floor by pulling in sides of soles

The sitting stance is often depicted as a stance that one adopts when standing in front of an opponent and punching them to the front (see Figure.55).

However, even an untrained person could point out the defensive flaws of such an approach. You are very open, quite immobile and liable to be pushed over or kicked in the groin. However, the sitting stance is one of the most useful stances and is a staple of the grappling arts. The table below details the stance through the prism of our three inherent qualities.

To best illustrate the properties of a sitting stance, let us look at three of its most common grappling uses:

1. The guillotine.
2. The Do-San takedown.
3. The 9-shaped arm bar (covered earlier).

Figure 55: The vulnerability of attacking in sitting stance

Stability	• Highly stable in two directions: downwards and sideways • Very wide base and very low centre of gravity. Therefore, ideal for holding and dragging down opponents • Very short length so easy to off balance to the front or the back • Stability issues easily rectified by attaching oneself to opponent and so increasing your base from 2 feet to 3 or 4
Mobility	• It is incredibly stable and so is inherently immobile. Removing one foot from the floor in such a low and wide stance will inevitably result in a fall. However, small shuffles to make adjustments to combative demands are very possible and may result in a diagonal stance or a Shiko Dachi, which has feet splayed.
Energy Transfer	• The ability to drop mass and centre of gravity makes downwards the best direction. This can be used to attack an opponent's balance • Lifting with large leg muscles and flexing spine can also be used to generate power • Punching and striking to the front is possible but lacks devastating power because mass is anchored in stance and can neither be projected forward nor sufficiently rotated

Sitting stance: Application A - The guillotine (Po–Eun Tul)

This is without doubt the easiest and most frequent type of standing choke. Variations of it can be seen in many of the Chang-Hon patterns, including Po-Eun and Yoo-Sin. It is achieved when one fighter suddenly bends over and the other encircles the neck with an arm (see Figure.56). It can be further achieved with one arm in or both arms out and can have a variety of hand and wrist configurations. However, what is consistent throughout all is:

- the radial bone of the forearm is pressed into the throat and, preventing breathing and crushing the trachea;
- the weight is dropped down through the opponent to break their posture; and
- the feet are spread wide to maintain downward pressure and to create stability.

Figure 56: The guillotine choke in sitting stance

Note: In this application, splaying the feet into a Shiko Dachi is preferred.

The steps

1. The defender is attacked with a hook punch, which is blocked with a KHGB.
2. The attacker is kneed in the groin or midriff to bend them over and expose the back of the neck.
3. The defender saws his arm across the neck of the attacker, maintaining constant downward pressure and dropping his weight down through the attacker by adopting a sitting stance.
4. The defender circles his arm under and across the throat of the attacker and secures his choking hand in his other hand.
5. The radial bone is now squeezed into the throat of the attacker and added pressure applied by the defender flexing his spine.

Sitting stance: Application B - Knife hand takedown (Do-San Tul)

In this technique, the sitting stance is used to attack someone's balance. Again, we drop weight down and through the opponent. However, in this example we also use the stance to block the feet of the opponent and prevent them from readjusting their base once we shift their centre of gravity away from it. This results in loss of balance and a takedown (see Figure.57).

The steps

1. The attacker's arm is lifted using a rising block. This disrupts their posture and momentarily prevents them from responding with proper power.
2. The defender spins round and under the arm to position himself behind the attacker.
3. With the defender now low in his stance and close behind the legs of the attacker, the attacker is prevented from stepping backwards in order to right his balance.
4. The defender can now apply backwards pressure using a knife hand across the chest to disrupt the balance of the attacker and take them down. This is further aided by the attacker using his knee to 'pop out' the knee of the attacker.

Figure 57: A takedown using a knife hand strike in sitting stance & an example of a 9-shaped block used as an arm bar (see Blocking chapter)

Sitting stance: Application C - 9-shaped arm bar (Gae-Baek Tul)

The 9-shaped arm bar has already been explained in the chapter on blocking. However, again we can see the use of the stance at work. The bent legs and wide base offer stability, and the height of the stance can be adjusted to suit the height of the opponent. Stepping in behind the oponent will stop them from turning to alleviate pressure on the elbow and to escape the lock.

2. Walking Stance

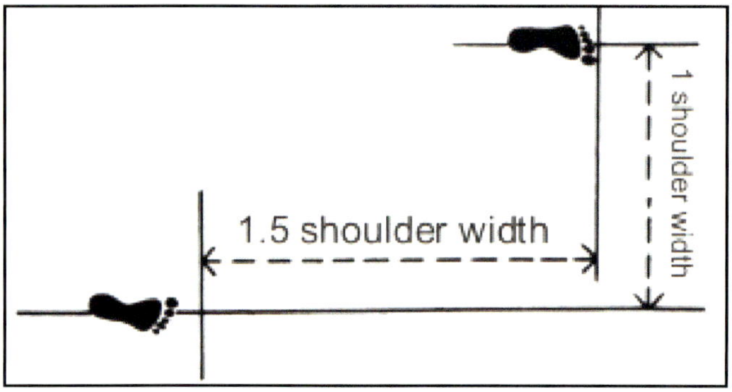

- Length is 1.5 shoulder width between big toes
- Width one shoulder from centre of each instep
- Front foot points forward; back foot points out at 25 degrees
- Front knee in line with heel; back leg straight
- Weight 50:50

The walking stance is most often depicted as being used to deliver a straight punch by stepping forward from outside engagement range. Whilst this application is distinctly possible, it is unlikely to be of much use in actual combat where the distance and time necessary to make it work are rare. However, the stance is of great use for projecting force forwards whilst holding on to an opponent. Therefore, a number of applications that require energy to be transferred through an opponent in a forward and perhaps downward motion favour this technique. One often-missed detail is the utility of the straight back leg. The rigidity of it ensures that when striking there is minimum recoil and so energy is not bled backwards but is rather efficiently concentrated forwards (Swanson, 2017). Though rarely commented on, the prop structure is often seen in boxing and MMA when fighters are throwing power punches. Indeed there are many photos of Iron Mike Tyson doing just that.

Walking stance vs front stance

Walking stances are modified versions of a Karate front stance, which has more weight on the front leg (60:40) than in Taekwon-Do (50:50). To create this extra emphasis on the front, the leg of a front stance has a more acute bend than the Taekwon-Do version (see Figure.58). Indeed, whereas in Taekwon-Do the knee is placed over the heel, in Karate it is positioned over the ball of the front foot.

However, Karate front stances are themselves modified to fit in with modern Karate dogma. In Funakoshi's 1935 version of *Karate do Kyohan*, the Master himself can be seen to have high stances that resemble our Taekwon-Do walking stance. However, in the 1973 reprint, the new photographs can be seen to adopt the longer and less mobile front stance commonly seen in Shotokan today.

Stability	• Very stable in four directions but vulnerable on the 45 degrees • Straight back leg works like a prop to resist pressure in this direction and prevent recoil
Mobility	• The higher the stance the more mobile it is • Easily adjustable to the side with a slight step • Straight back leg slows mobility forwards and backwards whilst in stance
Energy Transfer	• Extremely effective at projecting mass forward or backwards • Stance is considerably lower than standing, so rising and falling can project energy up and down • Rotational projection through stepping 90 degrees very effective, i.e. sajo jirugi • Hips can be adjusted to harness the core to generate more power • Straight back leg limits recoil on impact, thereby ensuring maximum projection of energy

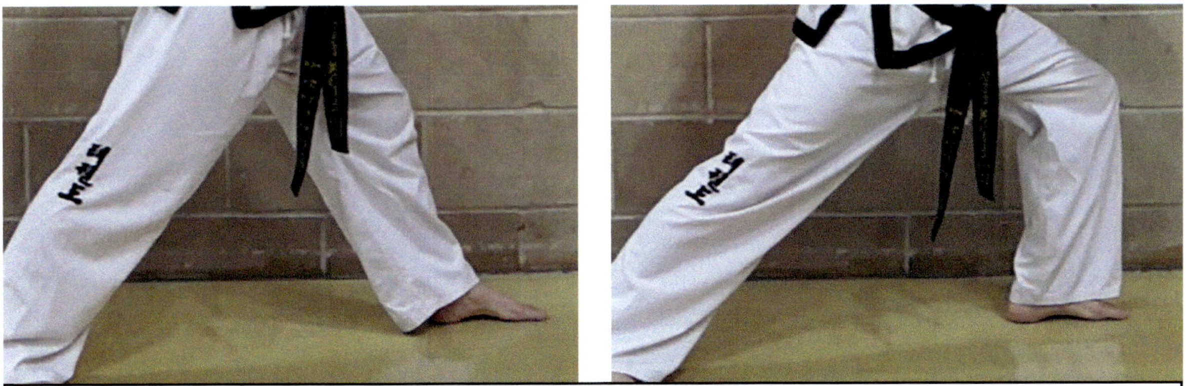

Figure 58: Contrast between a TKD walking stance and a Karate front stance, respectively

Walking stance: Application A - High reverse knife hand strike or ridge hand (Hwa-Rang Tul)

This technique uses the forward momentum of the attacker against them and in so doing generates a lot of destructive force. It is very similar to what a wrestler would call a 'clothes line' (see Figure.59). It is crucial that the technique is timed so that the attacker is still moving forwards when contact is made.

The steps

1. The attacker steps forward and raises an arm (i.e. punch, grab, poke with finger).
2. The defender turns offline and palms down the attacker's arm, exposing the throat and bringing the head forwards.
3. The defender projects his weight forwards into a walking stance and at the same time strikes into the throat with a ridge hand.
4. The defender can either follow up by kicking the downed opponent or simply disengaging.

Figure 59: Walking stance used to project weight forwards and maintain stability in attack

Note: The walking stance is an extremely common stance for a defensive template to finish in. Many takedowns and throws like o soto gari (pictured earlier) end in walking stance to regain balance. Further examples of the application of the walking stance can be seen by referring back to the Blocking chapter or by examining the applications of other stances detailed below.

3. Low Stance

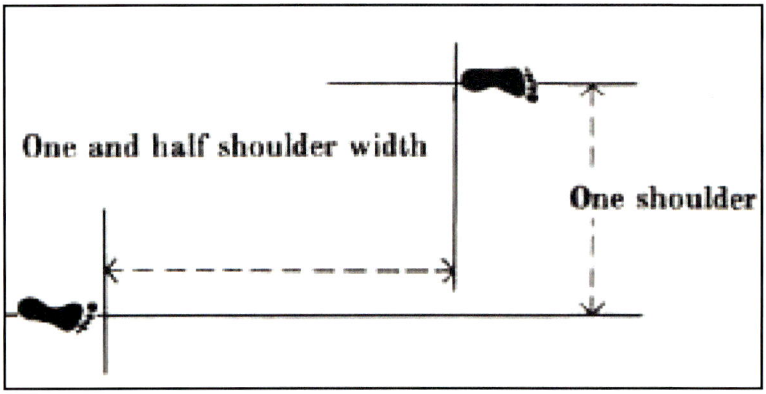

- Full facing or half facing
- One foot's length longer than a walking stance
- Said to offer opportunity to extend attacking tool longer
- Weight 50:50

Stability	• Very stable in four directions because of very low centre of gravity • Vulnerable on 45 degrees but because the purpose requires anchoring to an opponent and therefore extra stability, not really relevant
Mobility	• Very poor mobility because feet are so far apart that knee spring is difficult and lifting either foot without falling is tricky
Energy Transfer	• Downward pressure, forward pressure or both highly effective • Downward strikes possible because rising and falling of mass effective • Striking forward whilst in stance ineffective because mass anchored and body mechanics poor

Though rare, the low stance is really just a slightly longer walking stance with a very specific purpose: it is always used to control a fallen opponent. Therefore, in the patterns, low stances generally appear following a takedown or as part of a takedown. The extra length of the stance permits the user to remain in contact with the grounded opponent without the need to lean forwards and compromise balance. A good example can be seen in the arm bar takedown from the Joong-Gun Tul (see Application A below).

Low Stance: Application A - Arm bar takedown (Joong-Gun Tul)

This technique is seen in Joong-Gun Tul where it is performed as a palm pressing block (here it is done with the forearm). The low stance is used to remain in contact with the fallen opponent in order to retain control. The longer stance permits the defender to keep downward pressure without leaning forwards and sacrificing balance. If the opponent ends up prone on the floor then one can easily step in and control by using an x-stance to pressure shoulder and elbow simultaneously (see Figure.60).

The steps

1. The defender is grabbed by the lapel.
2. The defender reaches over and grabs holds of the attacker's grabbing hand, securing it to his clothing, all the while conscious of the attacker's free hand.
3. The defender distracts the attacker (flick testes, low kick, spit, knee, punch, poke in eye, etc.) and turns 90 degrees, thereby twisting the arm of the attacker to point the elbow up.
4. The defender places his free hand on the back of the attacker's elbow and exerts downward pressure whilst maintaining a secure hold of the attacker's grabbing hand in its original position.
5. The defender maximises the downward pressure through the attacker's elbow by drop ping body weight low as a low stance is adopted.
6. The attacker must go to the ground to avoid damage to the elbow.
7. The defender maintains control on the ground or strikes and disengages.

Figure 60: A low stance used to maintain control of a downed opponent without sacrificing balance. Also an X-stance used to pressure elbow and shoulder simultaneously (see above).

4. L-Stance

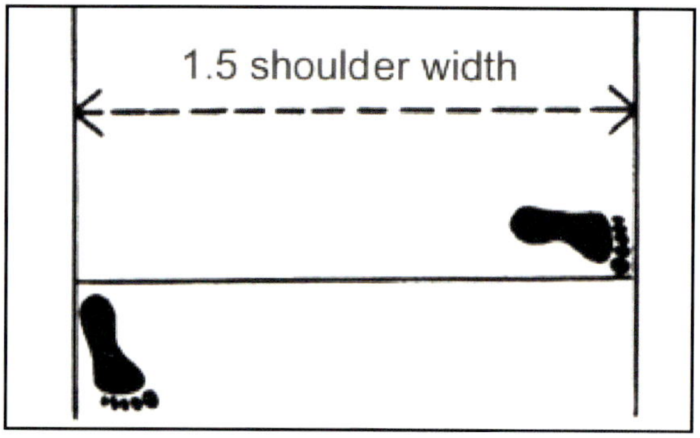

- Weight 70:30 with most on back leg
- 1.5 shoulder widths in length from front toes to back foot sword and 2.5cm between heels
- Back knee over back ball of foot
- Back hip in line with inner knee joint
- Both feet turn in 15 degrees

Stability	• Very stable forwards and backwards due to low centre of gravity • Not hugely stable sideways but the 2.5cm greatly increases stability from feet directly in line • Both legs bent facilitates easy adjustment on demand
Mobility	• Extremely mobile because both legs are bent and can push in either direction • 15 degrees on back foot, which permits back leg to project to front as well as sideways
Energy Transfer	• Bent legs make energy transfer forwards and backward very effective because large muscles of the legs are utilised • Half facing posture of stance allows torque through trunk and core • Sinking down or corkscrewing down can both be utilised to create power in strikes and grappling • Often used to project all mass forwards by slipping from this stance to a walking stance or fixed stance (see above)

This is a truly multi-purpose stance and its uses typify the dichotomy of the split between the old grappling-based strategies of old school Karate and the more modern mobile striking practices of Taekwon-Do. It is so effective at delivering strikes and moving that versions of it can be seen in nearly all combat arts: boxing, fencing, MMA, Karate, Escrima to name but a few. However, the semi-circular movement of the feet means that the defender can step in close behind an opponent and is then able to use the legs to block or attack those of the opponent.

L-Stance: Application A - Shifting from L-stance to walking stance (Joong-Gun Tul)

This example shows the ability of the L-stance to shift mass around and create huge amounts of power. By using the bent back leg of the L-stance, one is able to effectively drive mass forwards whilst slipping the front foot and adopting a longer stance (see Figure.61).

The steps

1. The attacker throws a hook punch, which is blocked with a KHGB in L-stance.
2. The defender wraps the attacker's arm in order to create a hikite (pulling hand), which will pull the attacker on to the counter.
3. The defender slips his front foot into a walking stance and drives his elbow up into the jaw of the attacker. The force is maximised by pulling the attacker on to the elbow with the hikite.

Figure 61: Using bent back leg to drive mass forward into an upward elbow in walking stance
Note: The defender's hand wraps the attackers arm to create a pulling hikite (KHGB pictured)

L-stance: Application B - Knife hand strike (Dan-Gun Tul)

This strike is often misunderstood and is usually interpreted to take place from an ineffective distance. However, when used in grappling range, the strike again utilises the hikite to maximise striking power (see Figure.62). This time, the 45-degree angle of the L-stance is used to stretch out the attacker and disrupt their posture whilst retaining the ability to step forwards and strike.

The steps

1. The defender somehow manages to secure a cross grip of the attacker's wrist.
2. The defender does a number of things at exactly the same time:

- pulls the attacker's wrist to his hip and disrupts the attacker's posture to expose the neck;
- steps in behind the attacker's leg to block it; and
- executes a knife hand strike to the throat.

Now the defender is in a vulnerable position and can be dispatched with one of two alternative exits:

1. The defender can step in and land an easy punch to the exposed jaw of the attacker; or

2. The defender can use his front leg to pop the knee of the attacker and, by continuing the push-pull motion of the knife hand hikite, the attacker will lose his balance and a take-down will be effected.

Figure 62: The L-stance used to step in behind and strike. It can be used to project mass forward or to pop a knee for a takedown.

5. Fixed Stance

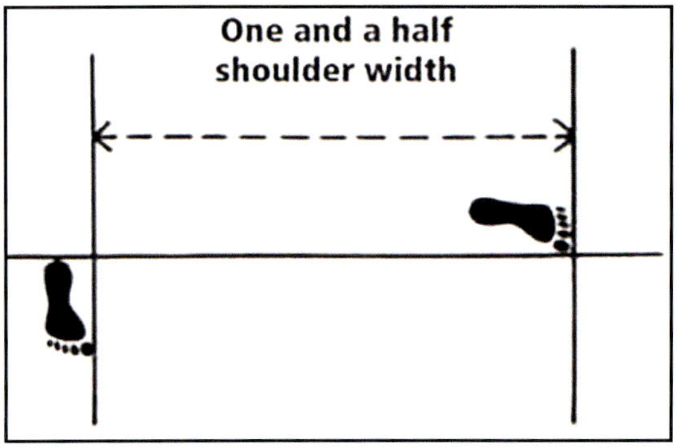

- Similar to L-stance but weight 50:50
- 1.5 shoulder width in length between big toes on either foot
- 2.5cm width between heels
- Both feet turn in 15 degrees

The fixed stance is generally, though not always, used when the defender is currently in an L-stance and is holding on to an opponent. The anchoring to the opponent makes walking forward (TKDers' favoured method of creating power) impossible and so, to project mass forwards and into the technique or opponent, the defender transitions to a slightly longer stance. Because the mass (i.e. the body) is moving forward and the stance is longer, the body moves from its back-leg base to a more central position. Therefore, the weight distribution changes to accommodate this (i.e. from 70:30 to 50:50). Unlike the sitting stance, the fixed stance has the hips at roughly 45 degrees and so is half facing and can utilise the mobility of the core to generate huge power from the transition of the stance. This can be used to turn into an opponent. All applications of the fixed stance involve holding on to an opponent and take place at grappling range. Most use the legs of the fixed stance to block those of the opponent. Most also involve a shift into this stance from sitting or L-stance.

Stability	• Like the L-stance, the fixed stance is very stable in one direction owing to its long base. However, its lack of width makes it relatively unstable width-ways. • Stability is usually created by attaching oneself to an opponent and therefore becoming four legs rather than two
Mobility	• Very poor mobility because weight is low and central, making lifting either leg problematic • Stance usually only travels forwards, not backwards, and usually does so by slipping from an L-stance • Slight shifting of the feet is possible to adjust balance
Energy Transfer	• Projecting mass forwards and downwards creates huge power • Torqueing of body possible, which increases efficiency of transference of energy

Fixed stance: Application A - Pulling arrows (Won-Hyo Tul)

These three moves come from Itosu's Karate kata Heian Yondan. Here, we can see the shift from the L-stance into the fixed stance in order to apply force in that direction. Though the fixed stance in this application can be used for a strike, it is also used to stretch out the opponent in a move know as 'pulling arrows' (see Figure.63).

The steps

1. The attacker has the defender secured in a lapel grab. As such, the defender need only worry about one arm, which is **likely** to come in a hook punch or a head butt. The defender raises both hands to deal with the threat.

2. As the attacker throws his circular punch, the defender forms a twin forearm block. However, the defender simultaneously uses the front hand to punch the face of the attacker.

3. The defender then uses his front arm to strike into the forearm of the defender's grabbing arm and folds it. This will twist the posture of the attacker and expose his/her neck. At the same time, the defender chops into the now exposed neck of the attacker.

4. The attacker reaches over to secure the defender's grabbing arm and stop him/her read-

justing his/her posture.

5. The defender shifts his weight on to his back foot momentarily and projects it sideways whilst punching the exposed jaw of the attacker.

6. As the arm of the defender is still attached and controlled, the punch has the effect of stretching him/her out in a posture known as pulling arrows. A cursory glance at the posture will confirm both how effective it is at control and how it resembles that of an archer readying for a shot.

7. By puffing out one's chest the attacker's arm can be barred and the elbow joint attacked.

Figure 63: Using the fixed stance to stretch out an opponent and bar (pulling arrows)

6. X-Stance

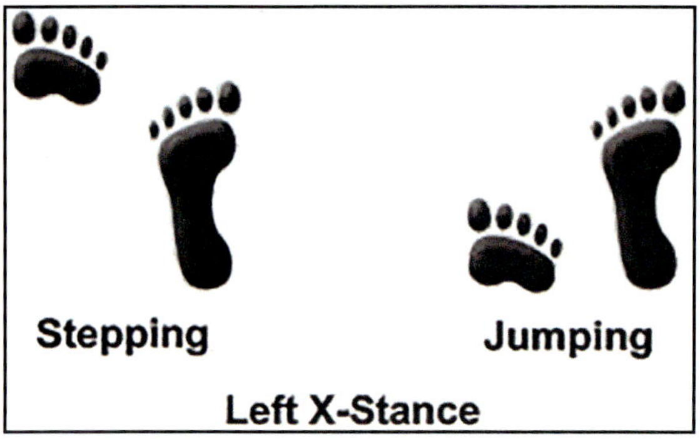

- Body weight on stationary foot
- One foot crossed over or behind the other, touching the ground with the ball of the foot
- For stepping: front foot makes crossing motion across back foot
- For jumping: back foot makes crossing motion behind front foot

This stance is one of the most confusing. It is usually misconstrued as a method of striking (back fist mostly) by jumping and the emphasis in patterns is always placed on balancing in a static position. As such, it is of little use because it lacks stability and penetrating power. Furthermore, tying the legs up creates both mobility and balance issues. However, by looking at other combat arts, for example, MMA, Judo and classical Ju Jitsu, we can see that the same configuration of feet appears in highly practical applications. Indeed, one of the properties of the stance that is often missed is its ability to rotate to uncross the legs. This huge twisting/spinning motion is very useful when attempting to move an opponent or when used against an opponent who is trying to restrict your movement.

Another aspect that is misunderstood is the way in which the legs get into the cross position. This movement in itself can be used as a method of attacking an opponent's balance. The most important thing to remember is that the X-stance is a transitory position and spending too much time in the position itself will make the defender vulnerable in all manner of ways, so it **must** be transitioned through rapidly to effect the defender's goals.

Stability	• Very poor because centre of gravity is very high and base is very small • Lack of stability means this position must be transitioned through rapidly to reduce vulnerability.
Mobility	• Rotating to untie the legs is practically the only movement permitted while in the stance
Energy Transfer	• Projecting mass forward at the cost of balance is possible and even desirable at times • Rotating whole body out of the X-shape can generate a huge amount of power, which can be used in many ways

X-Stance: Application A - Set up for a shoulder throw (Yul-Gok Tul and Gae-Baek Tul)

This application uses the stance as a set-up for a throw (see Figure.64). As such, the twisting motion of the transition uses the torque to disrupt the opponent's balance. The second linked use is to pressure the shoulder to maintain control of a downed opponent (see Figure.65).

Figure 64: X-stance used as a set-up for a throw. Grips on elbow and collar of garment

The steps

1. The defender manages to gain a good grip on the garment of the attacker, i.e. sleeve at the elbow and high collar (NB: similar throws can be done without garments).

2. The defender steps into the attacker's personal space, making sure to keep his hips lower than the defender's and to maintain maximum body contact (NB: to distract the attacker, the defender can slam his body into the attacker's to knock the wind out of him. However, it is essential that the attacker is not projected away and that body contact is not lost).

3. As the attacker is loaded on to the shoulder and hips of the defender, the defender simply untwists his feet to effect a shoulder throw.

X-Stance: Application B - Shoulder lock for ground control (Toi-Gye Tul)

Figure 65: A shoulder lock using X-stance

The steps

1. If the fallen opponent remains on his side or front after the fall, the defender can quickly step in and use the knee of his back foot to press into the depression between the shoulder and the humerus bone and keep the attacker pinned to the floor. Doing so will raise the heel of the foot off the floor to form an X-stance.

2. By twisting and straightening the attacker's arm and pinching it between the legs, the defender can use the back leg quad/thigh as a fulcrum to bar the arm and exert pressure on the elbow (NB: a wrist lock is also possible if desired).

X-Stance: Application C - Escape from underhooks or bear hug (Eui-Am)

When an opponent grabs you in either a bear hug or gets what grapplers refer to as double underhooks, there is always a danger that they will pick you up and either carry or throw you. This technique uses the bending stance to prevent this by attaching oneself to the attacker. As the attacker cannot lift his/herself thus, this threat is negated. This technique appears in Karate kata Bassai where it is commonly an opening move (see Figure.66).

The steps

1. The attacker has double underhooks. To avoid being lifted the defender chops into the back of the attacker's leg hooking it.

2. The defender forms an augmented backfist and presses it into the facial nerve, which can be accessed under the cheek bone.

3. As the defender's posture is disrupted a takedown is affected by driving through the attacker. The defender now forms an x-stance to avoid falling.

Figure 66: Using a bending stance and an X-stance to escape from front underhooks (or bear hug)

7 and 8: Bending Stance and One-Leg Stance

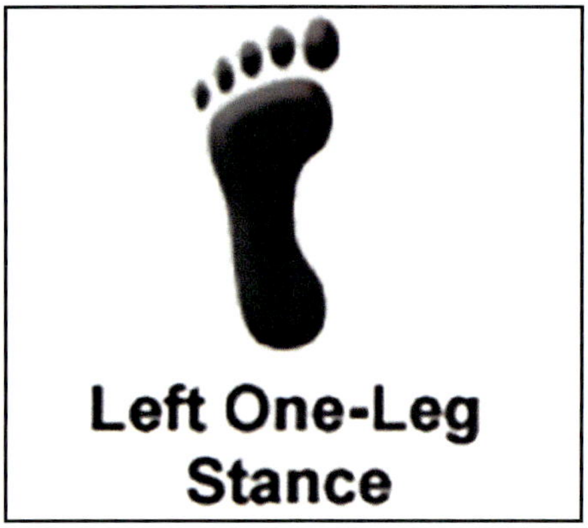

- One leg supports all weight
- One foot is flat on the floor while the other covers knee joint
- Supporting leg is bent in bending stance
- Supporting leg is straight in one-leg stance
- Stance is either full facing or half facing

The bending stance is very misunderstood and so its applications are overlooked. It is generally used as a preparatory stance for kicking. Though this is often correct, it is the distance and target of the kicks that are often wrongly attributed. Over the years, the heights of most kicks have been raised. This means that we now aim sidekicks at the middle section as opposed to attacking the knees, shins, feet and groin, as originally intended by the Okinawans. Obviously, attacking above the waist requires more range and is less likely to occur when an opponent is holding you. Furthermore, the way the bent leg travels to the knee is majorly overlooked. This is often a method of attacking the opponent by sweeping a foot or hooking a leg. The bending of the leg in a bending stance can be seen as a method of dropping weight down and through an opponent.

The one-leg stance is almost identical in its use to the bending stance. However, instead of lowering mass it raises mass. This can then be used to strike upwards with the knee or to lift and move an opponent and render them susceptible to throwing or further manipulation.

Stability	• Very poor because base is only one foot • It is essential to hold on to an opponent to avoid falling
Mobility	• Very poor because impossible to shift weight from one foot to the other • Hopping is the only method of movement available
Energy Transfer	• Whilst in the stance, it is only really possible to effectively transfer energy using the raised leg without compromising balance • The action of raising the leg itself can be used to pull and push opponent simultaneously as in bending ready stance A or to strike with knee as in one-leg stance

Bending stance: Application B - Sweep, knee press and elbow (Yul-Gok Tul)

This application takes place in a clinch. This is a commonplace for two fighters to find themselves once they are too close to strike. In such a position, even a little bit of knowledge offers a huge advantage. This application is seen in numerous Karate kata in one form or another (Heian Yondan, Arakaki Seisan, Hakutsuru and numerous others). In this version the bending stance uses the sweeping motion as the leg is drawn to the knee in order to sweep a leg (see Figure.67). Unlike most sweeps, this is not used to take the attacker down but rather to make his/her stance very wide and immobile. This makes it impossible for the attacker to lift either leg and so attacking the legs by kicking them becomes an effective way of turning their head in order to deliver a coup de grace to the selected vulnerable area; in this case, an elbow to the side of the head. A kick used in this manner is typical of old school Karate where most kicking was below the **waist.** . One interesting point is that the type of kick used tends to vary from style to style. It is not uncommon to see the knee attacked in this manner using a twisting kick, a side kick, a snap kick or a front thrusting kick. This is also a template that appears readily in clinch situations in competitive MMA.

The steps

1. The defender and attacker have ended up in a clinch. The defender is controlling the attacker's head with one arm whilst placing his own head to the other side to reduce vulnerability to the attacker's free arm. The defender controls the attacker's other arm with an over-hook, which pins it and negates risk from it.

2. The defender pulls the attacker to the right. The attacker steps this way to avoid falling and so momentarily transfers his/her weight mostly on to one foot. This makes his/her other foot very light.

3. The defender sweeps the attacker's light foot to create a very wide stance. Now the attacker cannot lift either foot without falling or readjusting.

4. The defender chambers a side kick and kicks out the inside knee joint of the unswept foot. This action will twist the attacker's body and expose the side of his/her head/jaw.

5. The defender secures the head of the attacker with one hand and projects his weight forwards and into an elbow strike in walking stance (NB: the hammer and anvil approach to striking is far more destructive than simple punching because it prevents recoil of the head. The difference is like kicking a cardboard box and stamping on it).

Figure 67: The sweeping motion of the bending stance used to move an opponent's leg in order to remove mobility and create an opportunity to attack the knee joint

9. Rear-Foot Stance

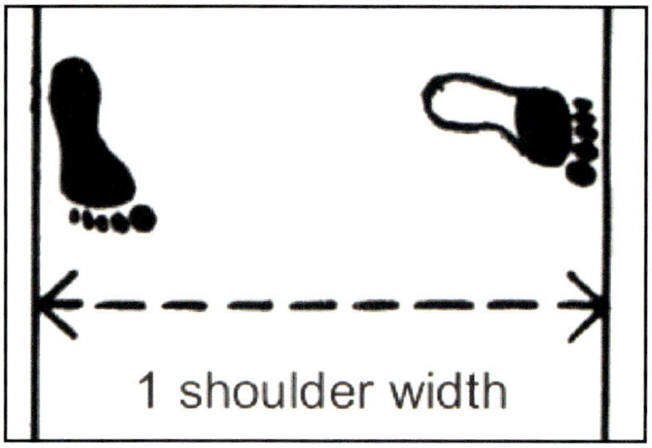

- 1 shoulder width in length between the small toes
- Heel of rear foot slightly beyond heel of front foot
- Rear leg bent with knee over toes, front leg bent with only ball of foot touching ground
- Back foot turns 15 degree and front foot 25 degrees
- Weight mostly over back foot (sometimes stated as 90:10)

This stance is used predominantly for one of two things:

1. dragging someone backwards; and
2. creating a seesaw effect to transfer maximum energy in an upwards direction.

The properties of the stance are such that one is able to drop nearly all one's weight over the back leg. This makes the front leg light and it can therefore be used for kicking or lifting and evasion of kicks/sweeps, i.e. Thai boxing. The movement of nearly all one's mass backwards and downwards at the same time can be used to drag things in much the same way as a person pulls a rope in a tug of war. Furthermore, the dropping down on the back leg can be used to catapult up the front hip, making a seesaw-type lever, which can be used to exert pressure to joints in an upwards motion. However, it should be highlighted that this stance is very often used in old school Karate as a method of stepping off line and blocking (i.e. middle block or KHGB). In such a use, the lack of weight on the front foot permits continual motion through stepping and sliding and a seamless transition from block to strike.

Stability	• Very stable in only one direction where it is able to resist being pulled forward • Poor stability in all other directions due to very small base
Mobility	• Lifting back leg is impossible owing to 90% of weight upon it. However, pivoting on back foot is easy and the option to lift and replace the front foot is always present
Energy Transfer	• Exploding forwards can transfer a huge amount of energy because back leg is very bent and can project nearly all mass forwards with great velocity • Shifting most mass backwards can drag heavy weights back and down • Seesaw and corkscrew effect of hips whilst dropping into stance can project energy upwards and forwards at velocity

Rear-foot stance: Application A: Upward palm block used to dislocate an elbow (Joong-Gun Tul)

This application uses the seesaw motion created when sinking into the stance in order to project force upwards and to transfer energy in that direction. The application uses an upward palm block to attack the elbow joint (see Figure.68). This is a much more feasible use of the 'block' than the proposed one of 'lifting a punch a few inches'. Unlike the pressing block application, the intention here is to destroy the joint. For this reason the action is done vigorously.

The steps

1. The attacker extends a hand towards the defender's face.
2. The defender turns offline and parries the attacker's hand.
3. The defender then uses the parry/jam system of the middle block and circles his hand up to disrupt the posture of the attacker and retain control of the attackers arm.
4. The defender quickly kicks out the knee of the attacker.
5. The defender uses the confusion to reach over and secure a grip of the attacker's wrist.
6. The defender simultaneously twists the wrist like a motorcycle throttle in order to turn the elbow down, and steps forward.

7. While stepping forward the defender uses an upward palm block to attack the elbow and separate the joint. It is the throwing forward of the hip and the corkscrew motion of dropping the weight that creates the pressure necessary to destroy the elbow joint.

Note: The palm or the forearm are both good tools for attacking the elbow in this manner.

Figure 68: Using the see saw action of the rear-foot stance to create upward force and attack the elbow joint

Rear-foot stance: Application B - Low double palm block as a wrist lock (Chong Jang Tul and Sam Il Tul)

This technique uses a wristlock called a 'kotegaeshi' in Japanese. It is a lock that is extremely popular in Aikido, where it is used to subdue or throw. Though it can be done with one hand, here both hands are utilised in order to increase control. In this application, one can see that the rear-foot stance is used to apply pressure in a downward motion whilst dragging the opponent backwards and hence down. It should be noted that, by adopting the rear-foot stance, the defender retains the ability to lift the front foot and so negates the attacker's ability to reach out and grab it to effect an escape.

The steps

1. The attacker grabs the defender's wrist in a same side grab.
2. The defender distracts the attacker by attacking the eyes. Immediately, he brings his forearm down and strikes into the forearm of the attacker. This will fold the attacker and bring his/her head forward.
3. The defender slides his hand down the attacker's arm and secures the hand.
4. The defender turns his body to twist the attacker's arm and wrist. As the attacker's grip is broken, the defender applies his second hand to the lock to add extra support.
5. The defender simultaneously hyper-flexes the attacker's wrist and drags it down and backwards.
6. With the attacker now crouching with one hand controlled and the other on the floor to prevent falling, the defender is easily able to kick to the face and follow up with a drop step punch.

Figure 69: Using a rear-foot stance to drag backward and apply a wristlock called a 'kote-gaeshi', which uses a low double palm block

10. Parallel Stance

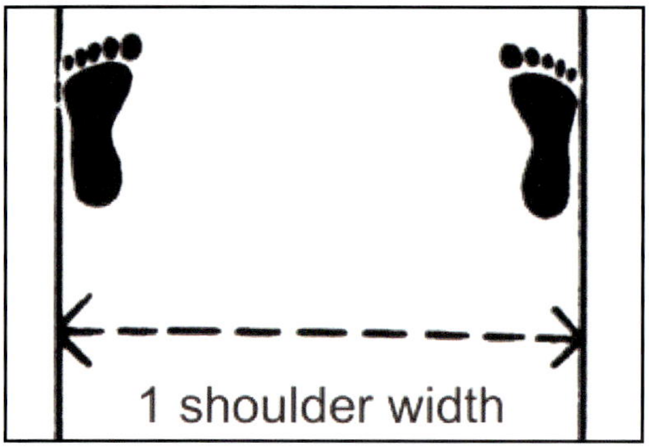

- Both legs straight though not locked
- Weight 50:50
- Full facing or side facing only
- Outside of feet parallel to shoulders with toes pointing forward

The parallel stance has both legs straight. Therefore, it is very high. It is full facing and open so none of the defender's vulnerable areas down the front of the body are protected. In such a position, the only place safe for a defender would be behind the attacker. Therefore, most of the applications for a parallel stance are ones where being high and being behind someone offer greater defensive qualities. However, one may find oneself in a parallel stance to the front if attacked in any number of common acts of violence, as follows:

- double lapel grab;
- two-handed strangulation;
- under arm bear hug from front;
- under arm bear hug from rear;
- over arm bear hug from front;
- over arm bear hug from rear;
- thrust against a wall;

- grab to the shoulder/s;
- hair pull;
- one-handed shove;
- two-handed shove;
- rear naked choke;
- rugby tackle from front;
- rugby tackle from rear;
- and many more...

Stability	• This is an extremely stable stance because it is a natural way of standing • Having the feet beneath the shoulders means that the weight is evenly loaded and adjustments to balance need only require small shifts of the feet
Mobility	• This is a very mobile stance because it is easy to shift weight on to a single leg at will • This is a natural position for walking. However, the straight legs make explosive movements difficult and limit lifting to just the arms.
Energy Transfer	• Because the legs are straight and parallel, the core is not greatly exploited in this stance. This means that generating power is limited. However, transitioning to another stance from this position is very easy and so the twisting and dropping of weight that such a movement requires can be used to transfer energy efficiently in any direction

Furthermore, most techniques that can be applied in a closed stance can also be applied in a parallel stance without much ill effect as both stances have:

- Straight legs;
- Weight evenly distributed; and
- Feet more or less under shoulders.

Examples of how one may be attacked in a parallel stance

Here are just a few examples of how one can be attacked while standing naturally in parallel stance. Obviously, one can see that most of these are control positions. A cursory glance at the parallel stance contained within the Chang-Hon Tuls will demonstrate that many of their applications are responses to these common acts of violence (see Figure.70).

Figure 70: Examples of common attacks one may encounter in parallel stance

Examples of simple escapes from common controls in parallel stance: Kwang-Gae, Ko-dang/Ju-Che, Choong-Jang, Choong-Moo, Toi-Gye, Gae-Baek Tuls (and many others)

Once an opponent grabs you, they have committed their hand/hands to controlling you. This means that they have effectively reduced their ability to strike you with their hands. They also

Figure 71: Attacking the fingers; attacking the eyes; attacking the ears; attacking the throat; attacking the elbows; attacking the temple or pressure points behind the ears.

have reduced their ability to prevent you striking them. Therefore, with a small amount of knowledge, the defender should be able to attack the vulnerable areas of the body and escape from the control position. Attacking the hands, throat, eyes, groin, ears and numerous pressure points around the body are very effective ways of achieving this, examples of which can be seen in nearly every tul (see Figure.71).

Attacking the opponent from behind (Toi-Gye, Joong-Gun & Eui-Am Tuls)

As previously stated, standing behind an opponent is a good place to be. It dramatically reduces their ability to both see you and effectively hit you. It also provides great mechanical advantage to the defender and offers all manner of control opportunities. Here, the parallel stance can be utilised for height because the opponent is pulled backwards and down to disrupt his/her balance and possibly choke. Opposite are just a few that can be found in the patterns (see Figure.72).

Figure 72: Parallel stance attacks: punching the chin; choking using the garment; cranking the neck; hair and arm control; rear naked choke

11. Vertical Stance

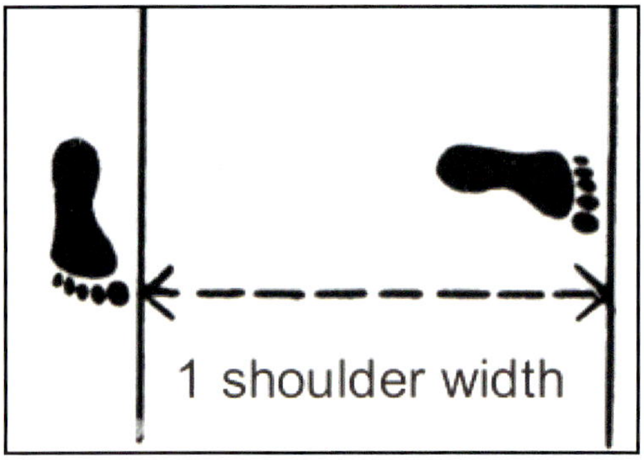

- One shoulder width between the big toes
- Both feet turn in at 15 degrees
- Weight distribution is 60:40 with most on the back leg
- Both legs are straight
- Stance is always half facing in both attack and defence

Stability	• This is an extremely stable stance because it is a natural way of standing when turned to look sideways • Having the feet beneath the shoulders means that the weight is distributed well (60:40) and adjustments to balance need only require small shifts of the feet • The straight back leg acts like a prop to halt backward motion
Mobility	• Though mobility is possible in this stance the straight back leg is there to stop backward movement and thus reduces explosion • Forward movement is generally seen after drawing the body backward into this stance
Energy Transfer	• Body is turned at 45 degrees so the core can be utilised but the position of the feet make generation of power tricky whilst in the stance However, transitioning to another stance (i.e. walking) provide a solution to this issue

The vertical stance in the Chang-Hon patterns is usually accompanied by a slight backwards movement, i.e. transitioning from a longer stance to the more upright and shorter vertical stance. Such a backward motion can have the effect of dragging an opponent who is connected to you and momentarily distracting them with temporary loss of balance. The stance is rare in the patterns and is nearly always associated with a circular and downward action of the arm.

Vertical stance: Application A - Centre lock (S-lock) against cross shoulder grab (Hwa-Rang Tul)

This is an extremely painful wristlock and one of the most effective in the Taekwon-Do canon. It relies on the arm of the attacker being bent and the elbow being lower than the wrist. Though mostly applied using the hands, this version uses the elbow and is therefore extremely powerful and dangerous (see Figure.73). This template can be seen in Karate kata Heian/Pinan Shodan (sometimes called Heian/Pinan Nidan in some styles). Though in Taekwon-Do and some forms of Karate the reaction hand retracts to the hip when executing the downward strike, in many other styles the reaction hand remains on the chest in the region where the pectoral muscle meets the deltoid. The hand remains in this position because it is clamping something to the body of the defender (in this case the attacker's hand). This wristlock is extremely painful and can also be used against a grab from behind to great effect (Aragaki Seisan).

The steps

1. The attacker's shoulder is grabbed in a cross grab. The defender reaches across with the opposite hand and clamps the attacker's hand to his own body.

2. The defender circles his arm up from underneath the attacker's and brings his elbow down on the wrist of the attacker. If done with control, this forms an effective centre lock. If done quickly, it will break the wrist.

3. As the attacker bends and drops to relieve the pressure on his wrist, he exposes the side of his jaw.

4. The defender secures a hold of the attacker's clothing and steps in to punch the now exposed jaw.

5. The defender reaches round the face of the attacker to grab his chin.

6. In a big stepping motion, the defender pulls the chin of the attacker round in a whipping motion to affect a takedown.

Note: The takedown here is done using exactly the same motion as a low block in walking stance i.e. Chon-Ji Tul.

Figure 73: Backward movement into vertical stance used to apply a centre lock (with takedown follow)

So to summarise:

To summarise, in modern arts such as Shotokan and Taekwon-Do, stances have become synonymous with stance training. Dedicating many hours to achieving the perfect position and posture has become the purpose of this and such arts have lost focus on the utility of each stance and the unique properties that make it functional. Many martial artists seeking 'real' self-defence have rightly concluded that time could be better spent learning 'actual' combat rather than focusing on aesthetics. This has wrongly caused many to conclude that the stances themselves have no value. However, stances exist in all sports, and any golfer, shot putter or fencer will be able to attest to the need to be able to adopt a good stance. Stances are basic devices to deliver force or to negotiate it.

The main properties of a stance are: stability, mobility and transference of energy. Though all of these properties are desirable, they are not equally achievable. Therefore, each stance can be seen as a trade-off between stability and mobility. The transference of energy will be affected too by the proportions of these inherent qualities. By looking at the 13 major stances, we can see how the postures adopted offer a unique combination of the three qualities of stability: mobility and energy transfer and how each application exploits the specific characteristics of its stance to effect its outcome.

To conclude, one can see from a cursory glance at the multiple applications detailed above that stances are essential tools to respond to the dynamic demands of violence. Because the intention and strategies used to negotiate violence change, so does the stance one selects. Common responses to violence such as blocking, striking, kicking, throwing, resisting, pulling, pushing, escaping, controlling, and strangling place different demands on the body. Therefore, the posture (stance) adopted for each technique must change to reflect this. As such, the selection of the correct stance will be determined **not** by what it looks like but rather by its ability to facilitate one's purpose, i.e. to effectively negotiate violence.

Though modern Taekwon-Do is concerned more with what a stance looks like rather than what it is for (form over function), it should be remembered that violent aggressors do not care how close your stance is to the ideal model. In the reality of violent encounters, it is important to remember that you will transition through many stances and that the efficacy will be judged by how successful you are at surviving the attack or in dispatching the attacker. Remember Nakamura's wise words: "You don't fight in a stance; you finish fights in a stance."

태권도

Conclusion

So, after exploration of the three major elements of Taekwon-Do – the history of the patterns, the nature of blocking and the true use of stances – we can draw a number of important conclusions. The acceptance of these conclusions will permit us to fully exploit the great but often untapped resource of the Chang- Hon Tuls.

Conclusion1: Many patterns are derived from older Karate kata

After looking at the evidence, it is irrefutable that many of the templates (58%) were derived from older Karate kata. In fact, most of the templates come from the Pinan/Heian series, which were themselves created by distilling older, longer kata and recombining major templates into more teachable chunks. Though accepting this will be difficult for some, it should not be seen as weakening Taekwon-Do but rather offering it more than is currently available. By accepting that many of the patterns are older than the modern arts of Taekwon-Do and Shotokan Karate, we can sidestep their modern and often impractical interpretations of pattern applications. As a result, we permit ourselves to look for applications which are more realistic and deal with a greater range of violent techniques than the long-range punches and kicks that the standard explanations are based on.

By recognising the presence of close-quarter fighting techniques in the patterns, we can begin to reintroduce the types of applications for which they were originally intended. Therefore, the patterns become a rich collection of chokes, throws, escapes, control techniques, joint locks, pressure point strikes and more. When the patterns are fully exploited in this manner, the student becomes much more capable of dealing with the types of violence they may meet in a 'real' self-defence situation rather than in the highly ritualised practice of set sparring.

Conclusion 2: The history of Karate prior to 1955 is the history of Taekwon-Do

After establishing and admitting to ourselves that Taekwon-Do came from modern Karate, we are then able to share in the rich history and historical resources that belong to us all. Some examples include:

- Lost two-person training methods that were used to effectively drill the close-quarter techniques found in kata/tuls.
- The Bubishi, which is an ancient text on Kung-Fu and Karate secretly passed from master to master throughout history.
- Tales of the old masters. By analysing these texts and stories, we can get a real flavour for how they envisioned their art to be employed and consequently how much of ours may be used too.
- Trapping and sticking hands skills that build up sensitivity and therefore permit the fighter to transition between moves whilst retaining control.

Conclusion 3: Blocking in its current form is impractical and ineffective

After exploring the weird and wonderful world of 'classical' blocking, it is impossible to conclude anything other than what Bruce Lee did. Blocking is a 'classical mess'. Blocks don't work in their current form because they are misinterpreted and leave out important elements. The failure of many arts to explain and to utilise the 'chamber' position is the biggest problem. Once this essential stage in utilised as a parry (for middle, low and high blocks), rather than simply ignored, then the blocks begin to take on a new life and a new purpose. More to the point, they become effective and enrich our system rather than detract from it.

Conclusion 4: There are too many mislabelled blocks

As previously pointed out, most of the blocks are not in fact blocks at all but were incorrectly labelled as such by the Japanese and, through linguistic ambiguity, this has perpetuated until this day. Again, by accepting this we are free to seek the true nature of these techniques. If they are not blocks but something else, and we currently practise them, would it not make sense to find out what they are? Grappling applications that look just like many of our blocks can be seen in many arts. By bringing them back to Taekwon-Do, we offer the student new avenues of study that will keep them engaged and attending once the extreme physicality of Taekwon-Do is beyond them.

Conclusion 5: The purpose of stances is not reflected in 'stance training'

'Stance training' and 'training to use stances' are **not** synonymous. They have very different objectives and need to be taught accordingly. Traditional stance training with its focus on conforming to an ideal shape is an attempt to improve one's character through introspection and represents the 'Do' part of our art. However, it does not teach you how to use your stances in actual combat nor does it teach you how to use stances to best negate the threat posed by an aggressive attacker. Teaching the combative purpose of stances is rare in Taekwon-Do. However, by examining the attributes of each stance and applying them in a number of simple self-defence scenarios, one can begin to understand the true nature of stances. Stances are devices that are used to create stability, mobility and to deliver force. Utilised in this way, stances become essential positions through which the fighter transitions in a fight. All students' training should reflect this reality.

So, what does this all mean to the Taekwon-Do student? Everything, nothing or both. To those who have been waiting for such information, this book could mean the world. Many of us in Taekwon-Do have dedicated a large part of our lives to the art. Some of us have always had a niggling feeling that there was more to the art than we were given. Others were certain of this but never knew where to look to confirm their suspicions. If you are one of these people, then this book is for you. If you always wanted to find out what was missing from the art you loved but didn't want to go and study another art then this book is also for you! However, we need to be realistic. This book will not change much. There are too many people with too much invested in the status quo for the ideas and information in this book to have much of an effect on the greater Taekwon-Do world. It is far easier for many to ignore the impracticalities of their system and continue to use the safe environment of the dojang to perpetuate inaccurate representations of 'real world violence'. For many to accept they are wrong is difficult but to admit it to their students impossible. That is fine. Martial arts in general and Taekwon-Do specifically is a broad church. There is room in it for us all. Furthermore, there are many who practice Taekwon-Do who have no interest in self-defence or in the applications of the patterns. Though this may seem strange to many of us, it must be recognised that people do martial arts for reasons that are personal to them. Furthermore, the reason one takes up a martial art is often very different to the reason one continues to practise it.

This book is neither an attempt to convert people to my way of thinking nor an attempt to shake up the Taekwon-Do world. It is simply a resource for those who would like to look beyond the dogma that blinkers us and see the art from a critical perspective. It is not disloyal or destabilising to seek answers to questions. Critically evaluating information is merely the tradition of post-enlightenment thinking that Western epistemology is based on. Testing the rigour and validity of all claims is the basis of modern science. As General Choi claimed so often that Taekwon-Do was a product of science, should we not apply scientific standards to its claims? By asking difficult questions we will not undermine our art but guarantee its continued success through the type of evolution that General Choi envisioned. This book is an attempt to show the student that there is much more to their Taekwon-Do than they currently know. How can that be bad?

Taekwon

Ciaran McDonald M.A., M.Ed. (Lover of the great art of Taekwon-do)

Volumes 2 and 3 will examine the focus on many of the lost practices of old school Karate and how they pertain to Taekwon-Do. Topics covered will include:

- Joint locking
- Throwing
- Pressure points
- Escapes and counters
- Dual action blocks
- Modern assumptions vs historical predications
- Angles and positions of opponents
- Sticking hands and sensitivity drills
- Traditional supplementary strength and impact training
- The influence of the Bubishi
- And much more

Volume 2 out soon….

Bibliography

Abernethy, I. (2002) *Bunkai-Justu: the practical application of kata*. Cockermouth: Neth Publishing.

Abernethy, I. (2012) In conversation during a seminar in Swindon.

Anslow, S. (2004) 'An interview with Grandmaster Kong Young Il.' *Taekwon-Do and Korean Martial* arts, 9(10).

Anslow, S. (2006) *Ch'ang Hon Taekwon-Do Hae Sul: real applications to the ITF patterns.* Co. Mayo, Eire: Counterpoint Press.

Anslow, S. (2009) 'ITF Patterns: Who Wrote What'. Martial Arts Planet (Forum). [Online]. Available at: http://www.martialedge.com/articles/history/a-history-of-modern-taekwondo-part-1/ (Accessed on 10 October 2011).

Black Belt Wiki (n.d.) 'Karate Stances'. [Online]. Available at: https://blackbeltwiki.com/karate-stances (Accessed on 1 January 2019).

Burdick, D. (2011) 'The History of Modern Taekwon-Do: Part 1: Martial Edge'. [Online]. Available at: http://www.martialedge.com/articles/history/a-history-of-modern-taekwondo-part-1/ Accessed on 10 October 2011).

Burgar, B. (2003) *Five years one kata: putting the kata back at the heart of karate*. Unknown: Martial Arts Publishing.

Choi. H.H. (1959) 'Taekwon-Do Teaching Manual'. [Online]. Available at:https://historyoftaekwondo.org/2015/04/10/1st-ever-taekwon-do-book/ (Accessed on 25 January 2019).

Choi. H.H. (1965) 'Taekwon-Do: the art of self-defence'. [Online]. English version available at: https://www.scribd.com/document/249714942/Taekwon-Do-The-Art-of-Self-Defence-Choi-Hong-Hi-1965 (Accessed on 1 January 2019).

Choi, H.H. (1988) *Taekwon-Do: the Korean art of self-defence.* Canada: International Taekwon-Do Federation.

Choi, H. H, (2000) *Taekwon-Do and I, volume 1: Motherland: the land in turmoil*. Unknown.

Choi. H.H. (2000) In interview with *Taekwon-Do Times*. [Online]. Available at http://www.tkdweb.nl/taekwon-do/interview-generaal-choi-hong-hi/ (Accessed on 1 January 2019).

Clark, R. (2001) *Pressure Point fighting: a guide to the secret heart of Asian martial arts.* Boston, MA: Turtle Publishing.

Cohen, I. (2017) *Karate Uchina-di.* USA: Self published.

Croft, A. (2009) *Intermediate Shotokan Karate: unravelling the brown belt and first black belt kata.* Marlborough: Crowood Press.

Forest East Taekwon-Do (n.d.) 'Taekwon-Do History'. [Online]. Available at: http://forest-east-tkd.co.uk/TaeKwonDoHistory.html (Accessed on 1 January 2019).

Funakoshi, G. (1935) *Karate-Do Kyohan: the master text for the way of the empty-hand.* Reprinted 2005. Richmond, TX: Neptune Publishing.

Funakoshi, G. (1973) *Karate-Do Kyohan: the master text.* Tokyo: Kodansha International Ltd.

Funakoshi, G. (1975) *Karate-Do: my way of life.* Tokyo: Kodansha International.

Funakoshi, G. (1988) *Karate-Do Nyumon: the master introductory text.* Tokyo: Kodansha International.

Gae Baek Hosin Sool (n.d.) [Online]. Available at: https://www.tkd.cz/postoj.aspx?id=12 (Accessed on 1 January 2019).

Gillis, A. (2008) *A killing art: the untold story of Taekwon-Do.* Toronto: ECW Press.

Kane, L.A. & Wilder, K. (2009) *The little black book of violence.* Wolfeboro, NH: YMMA Publishing Centre.

Kang, W.S. & Lee, K-M. (1999). *T'aekwondo Hyondaesa.* (Modern History of Taekwondo). Seoul, ROK: Pogyong Munhwasa.

Knapp, N. (2009) *Kung Fu Grappling.* Santa Fe, NM: Turtle Publishing.

Madis, E.,(2002) 'The Evolution of Taekwondo from Japanese Karate' [Online]. Available at: http://www.kidokwan.org/articles/the-evolution-of-taekwondo-from-japanese-karate (Accessed on 10 October 2018).

Madis, E. (2003a) 'The Fighting Arts Website. Storming the Fortress: a history of Taekwondo (Parts 1-4)'. [Online]. Available at: http://fightingarts.com/reading/article.php?id=658 (Accessed on 10 October 2011).

Madis, E. (2003b) 'Kido Kwan Martial Art International: the evolution of Taekwondo from Japanese Karate'. [Online]. Available at: http://www.kidokwan.org/?page_id=1535 (Accessed on 10 October 2011).

McCarthy, P. (1987) *Classical Kata of Okinawan Karate*. Burbank, CA: Ohara Publishing.

McCarthy, P. (1995) *The Bible of Karate: Bubishi*. Boston, MA: Tuttle Martial Arts.

McCarthy, P. (1999) *Ancient Okinawan Martial Arts: Koryu Uchinadi 2*. Boston, MA: Tuttle Martial Arts.

McCarthy, P. (2012) In conversation during a two-day seminar in Galway, Eire.

McCarthy, P. (n.d.) 'The fighting arts. On Choki Motobu'. [Online]. Available at: http://www.fightingarts.com/reading/article.php?id=400 (Accessed on 1 January 2019).

McDonald, S. (2016) 'Being grounded in martial arts'. [Online]. Available at: https://medium.com/@stuartmcdonald_60154/being-grounded-in-martial-arts-5c9cadf669e1 (Accessed on 1 January 2019).

Miller, R. (2011) *Facing violence: preparing for the unexpected*. Wolfeboro, NH: YMMA Publication Centre.

Miller, R. (2012) In conversation at Genjitsu seminar with Andi Kidd. Swindon, UK.

Ouyang, Y. (1997) The elevation of Taekkyon from folk game to martial art. *The Journal of Korean Martial Arts*, 6. Erie, PA: Via Media Publishing.

Swanson, J.D. (2017) *Karate Science: dynamic movement*. Wolfeboro, NH: YMMA Publication Centre.

Thompson, G. (1997) *Dead or alive: the choice is yours*. Chichester: Summersdale.

Tigon Martial Arts (2019) 'Physics for martial arts: kinetic energy and speed. [Online]. Available at: https://tigonkarate.com/physics-martial-arts-kinetic-energy-speed/ (Accessed on 1 January 2019).

Trimble, A. & Morris, V. (1995) *Karate Kata Applications*. London: Ebury Press.

University of Leicester Taekwon-Do Club (2011) 'Historical perspective: beginnings'. [Online]. Available at: http://www.ultkd.net/tkd/history.html (Accessed on 10 October 2011).

Wikipedia (1) (2011) 'Karate'. [Online]. Available at: http://en.wikipedia.org/wiki/Karate (Accessed on 10 October 2011).

Wikipedia (2) (2011) 'Taekwondo'. [Online]. Available at: http://en.wikipedia.org/wiki/Taekwondo (Accessed on 10 October 2011).

Wikipedia (3) (2011) 'List of Shotokan techniques'. [Online]. Available at: http://en.wikipedia.org/wiki/List_of_shotokan_techniques (Accessed on 10 October 2011).

Wikipedia (4) (2011) 'Taekyon'. [Online]. Available at: http://en.wikipedia.org/wiki/Taekkyeon (Accessed on 10 October 2011).

Wikipedia (5) (2018) 'SPEAR System' [Online]. Available at: https://en.wikipedia.org/wiki/SPEAR_System (Accessed on 1/12/18).

Yang, J.M. (1982) *Shaolin Chin Na: the seizing art of Kung-Fu.* Burbank, CA: Unique Publications.

Yang, J.M. (2004) *Analysis of Shaolin Chin Na: Instructors Manual for All Martial Styles.* Boston, MA: YMAA Publications.

태권도

List of figures

List of Tables